May I Help You?

Learning How to Interact With the Public

Heide Spruck Wrigley

K. Lynn Savage
Consulting Author

Nick Kremer
Project Director

Consortium on Employment Communication
Project Sponsor

ADDISON-WESLEY PUBLISHING COMPANY

Reading, Massachusetts • Menlo Park, California • Don Mills, Ontario • Wokingham, England • Amsterdam • Bonn
• Sydney • Singapore • Tokyo • Madrid • Bogota • Santiago • San Juan

A Publication of the World Language Division

Editorial: Kathleen Sands-Boehmer and Jennifer Bixby

Manufacturing/Production: James W. Gibbons

Design and Illustrations: Rosedesign Associates

Cover Design: Gary Fujiwara

Photo Research: Merle Sciacca

Photo Credits: p. 1, Papa Gino's of America; p. 2, Guenther Zuern, Friendly Ice Cream Corporation, Mark Morelli, Dunkin' Donuts Corporate Training Dept., Photo courtesy of Sears, Roebuck and Co.; p. 5, Dunkin' Donuts Corporate Training Dept.; p. 19, Photo compliments of McDonald's; pp. 24-25, Ralph Turcotte; p. 31, Embassy Suites; p. 33, Sheraton Tara Hotels; p. 46, Friendly Ice Cream Corporation; p. 56, Photo courtesy of Sears, Roebuck and Co.; p. 59, Byron Bush, pp. 71 and 75, Mark Morelli; p. 76, Ralph Turcotte; p. 81, Friendly Ice Cream Corporation; pp. 83-84, Mark Morelli; p. 86, Guenther Zuern, Walgreen Company; p. 91, Holiday Inn; p. 93, Walgreen Company; p. 103, George Mastellone; pp. 105, 108, Ralph Turcotte; p. 129, Mark Morelli; p. 141, Delta Air Lines, Guenther Zuern, and Ralph Turcotte; p. 142, Guenther Zuern; p. 146, Ralph Turcotte; p. 150, Mark Morelli.

Cover Photo Credits: Mark Morelli, Dunkin' Donuts Corporate Training Dept., Ralph Turcotte, and Walgreen Company.

We also wish to thank the staff of the International Institute of Boston, Michael Gebremarian and the staff at the Four Seasons Hotel in Boston, and Mal's New York Style Delicatessen of Boston.

ISBN: 0-201-09943-8
CDEFGHIJ-AL-89

**Project Sponsor
with major funding from the
Ford Foundation**

The Consortium on Employment Communication began in 1983 with major funding from the Ford Foundation. The Consortium's goal is to link linguistic minorities with the workplace. The Consortium's activities include developing instructional resources, impacting public policy, training staff, and conducting research.

Director: Nick Kremer
Consortium on Employment Communication
Center for Career Studies
California State University, Long Beach
Long Beach, CA 90840
213-498-4680

Members

Rita Cepeda
State Chancellor's Office
California Community Colleges
Sacramento, CA

Vy Trac Do
Santa Ana College
Santa Ana, CA

Carlos Gonzales
Adult, Alternative, and Continuing Education
State Department of Education
Sacramento, CA

David Hemphill
San Francisco State University
San Francisco, CA

Autumn Keltner
Continuing Education Centers
San Diego Community College District
San Diego, CA

Than Pok
United Cambodian Community
Long Beach, CA

Dale Rezabek
State Council on Vocational Education
Sacramento, CA

K. Lynn Savage
Center's Division
San Francisco Community College District
San Francisco, CA

Karen Thaxton
San Diego Regional Employment Consortium
San Diego, CA

Chui Lim Tsang
Chinatown Resources Development Center
San Francisco, CA

Ford Foundation Representative: Patricia Biggers

Contents

Introduction to Basic Service Encounters

"May I Help You?"

INTRODUCTION

This course will teach the kind of English used in hotels, motels, fast-food outlets, restaurants, different kinds of stores, gas stations, repair shops, and other service places.

Many different kinds of people are taking this course.

Henry Liao owns a small watch repair shop. He wants to learn English so he can talk to his customers.

Emanuel Valdez would like to find work in a hotel. He needs to learn how to talk to hotel guests and hotel staff.

Phenesy Savthisouk is not sure yet what kind of work she wants to do. She thinks she would like to learn the kind of English that will help her to work with people.

Vi Tang is working in a bakery/donut shop. He wants to improve his English so he can buy his own shop later.

Isabel Garcia works in a Mexican restaurant. She wants to learn how to talk to her English-speaking customers.

Vanary Prom wants to open a repair shop with his brothers. He wants to learn how to explain in English what's wrong with appliances, like refrigerators, washing machines, or dryers.

Van Nguyen helps her father in his gas station. She needs to learn to understand customers who have problems.

Elizabeth Gorecki has just started working in a department store. She wants to know how to explain customer problems to her manager.

Kyun Choi wants to improve her English so she can ask questions when she goes shopping.

Bijan Razevi is a college student. His family owns a motel. He wants to learn more English so that he can manage the motel later.

Dong Le just graduated from high school. He wants to work in a fast food restaurant until he finds something better.

Comprehension Questions

Read the introduction one more time and answer the questions.

1. Who works in a department store? _____

2. Whose father owns a gas station? _____

3. Why does Kyun Choi want to learn English? _____

   _____

4. Who speaks Spanish? _____

5. How long does Dong Le want to work in a fast food restaurant? _____

   _____

6. Who plans to fix refrigerators in the future? _____

   _____

7. Where would Emanuel Valdez like to work? _____

   _____

8. What kind of repair shop does Henry Liao own? _____

   _____

9. Where would Phenesy Savthisouk like to work? _____

   _____

Discussion

1. Are the people in your group similar to the people described in the Introduction?
2. Why are your classmates taking this course?
3. What are their plans for the future?
4. Where would they like to work after they finish this course?
5. What kind of work experience have they had?
6. Would you like working with people? Explain your reasons.
7. Could someone in your class draw a picture of your group?

Chapter 1
Understanding What The Customer Wants

"That was three chocolate donuts, right?"

OVERVIEW

Many people would enjoy working with people, but they are afraid their English is not good enough. They should not worry. Many people who don't speak perfect English have jobs where they talk to customers every day. They sell food at fast food stands, wait on tables in restaurants, collect money in parking lots, provide repair services in customers' homes, help guests in hotels and motels, or work as clerks in stores. Here are some of the things they say:

1. That's five jelly-filled donuts. Anything else?

2. $3.75, please.

3. The diet soft drinks are against the back wall.

4. What would you like on your hamburger?

5. This is a very nice watch and it is on sale.

6. Would you like soup or salad with your dinner?

7. Let me check with housekeeping to see if your room is ready.

8. I'm sorry I'm late, but traffic on the freeway was backed up for miles.

9. I'm sorry. These copies are a little crooked. Let me redo them for you.

10. Sugar cone or regular?

All these people provide services to customers and their jobs are part of the service industry.

Comprehension Questions

Look at the Overview again.
In your opinion, where do the people in the pictures work?

1. _Donut shop or bakery_   **6.** _____

2. _____   **7.** _____

3. _____   **8.** _____

4. _____   **9.** _____

5. _____   **10.** _____

Discussion

1. Do you think that store clerks in the United States behave differently than store clerks in your country? Explain.

2. In your opinion, what is the difference between a good service person and a bad service person? Explain and give examples.

INTERACTING

In a Donut Shop

Understanding what a customer wants is not always easy, especially if the customer speaks fast or mumbles. Experienced service employees know what to do to make sure they "catch" what the customer is saying.

You will hear two different interactions between a customer and a clerk in a donut shop. Listen and decide if the clerks are doing a good job.

Interaction I: What else do you want?

What Is Your Opinion?

Circle the answer that you think is best.

1. The clerk had no problems. He did an excellent job serving the customer.
2. The clerk did a terrible job serving the customer.
3. The clerk had some trouble understanding the customer, but that's okay. He still did a good job.

Discuss your answer with the other people in your group and explain your reasons.

Comprehension Questions

1. Who is talking?
2. Where is the interaction taking place?
3. What does the customer want?
4. Does the clerk understand what the customer wants? Explain.
5. What does the customer say about the coffee?
6. Does the clerk explain where the lids are? What does he say?
7. When does the clerk explain where the cream and sugar are?
8. Does the clerk sound friendly and helpful?
9. How does the customer want her change? Why?
10. Does the clerk explain why he can't give the customer the change she wants? What does the clerk say?
11. Is the customer happy? Why or why not?
12. What should the clerk do better next time?

Interaction II: Can I get you anything else?

Comprehension Questions

1. What does the customer order?
2. What does the clerk do when the customer orders?
3. Does the clerk understand what the customer wants?
4. What does the clerk say?
5. The clerk says: "They (the buttermilk bars) are very good, aren't they?" Why does the clerk say that?
6. The customer orders three cups of coffee. What question does the clerk ask?
7. What does the clerk say about the lids and the sugar and milk for the coffee?
8. What does the clerk do before he adds up the price?
9. The customer wants his change a special way. What does he say?
10. What does the clerk say? Does he give a reason?

Let's Compare

Who does a better job, the clerk in Interaction I or the clerk in Interaction II? Explain the difference.

_____

_____

_____

Now It's Your Turn

May I Help You?

Service employees work in many places, not only in donut shops. Wherever they work, they are expected to be helpful and friendly. Good employees always double-check an order; that means, they make sure that they understand what the customer wants.

Choose a situation in a donut shop or a fast food restaurant. Practice the customer/clerk interaction. One student is the customer, the other student is the counter clerk. The counter clerk tries to be polite, friendly, and helpful. Remember what you learned from listening to the tape.

ROLES

Customer: Orders food
Asks questions about food

Clerk: Asks customer to repeat
Answers questions
Double-checks the order

Role Play Checklist

Watch other students play the role of guest and counter clerk. Is the counter clerk friendly, polite, and helpful? Circle *yes* or *no* and discuss your answers with the class.

1. Did the counter clerk repeat the food order? yes/no
Did he/she sound friendly? yes/no

2. Did the counter clerk double-check when he/she did not
understand something? yes/no
Did he/she sound polite? yes/no

3. Did the counter clerk ask about food to go? yes/no

4. Did the counter clerk give good explanations? yes/no
Did he/she sound helpful? yes/no

5. Overall, how did the counter clerk sound? Circle the answer that you think is best.

   a) at times friendly, at times a little impolite

   b) friendly and helpful

   c) unfriendly and uncooperative

6. What could the counter clerk do better next time?_____

_____

_____

_____

Match-Up

Good service employees usually repeat a customer's order to make sure that they understand exactly what the customer wants. If they are not sure what the customer said, they will ask questions to get the right information.

AT A CUSTOMER'S HOME

Customer: My refrigerator is leaking water and doesn't keep the food cold.

Repair person: I'm sorry. It does not keep the food cold and what else?

Look at the customer orders below and match them with the service employee response.

CUSTOMER ORDERS

_____ **1.** I'd like the New York steak rare, please.

_____ **2.** I'd like to make a reservation for dinner for four people at 7:45.

_____ **3.** Could you check my oil and my tire pressure?

_____ **4.** Please make sure that you collate these copies.

_____ **5.** We would like a double-scoop of banana, a single scoop of raspberry, and three colas.

_____ **6.** I would like to request a wake-up call for 6:50 tomorrow morning, please.

EMPLOYEE RESPONSES

a) That was 6:15, six-one-five, correct?

b) I'm sorry. Check your oil and what else?

c) I'm sorry. What kind of ice cream did you want?

d) I'm sorry. How would you like that prepared again?

e) You want them put in order, right?

f) I'm sorry, that's for four people at what time?

LEARNING THE LANGUAGE

Sometimes clerks may have trouble understanding what the customer is saying. They may have to ask the customer to repeat the order.

Part I: Asking "What Kind . . . ?"

To make sure that there is no misunderstanding, a service employee should always double-check an order.

In a donut shop, you often hear the following:

Customer: I'd like three chocolate donuts and five (mumble mumble) bars.

Clerk: That's three chocolate donuts, and what kind of bars?

Customer: Glazed buttermilk bars.

Clerk: Here you are, five glazed buttermilk bars.

Quick Practice

One person will be the customer; another person will be the service employee. The service employee should NOT look at the text. Work in pairs and follow the example.

AT A CHINESE RESTAURANT

Customer: I would like the (mumble mumble) rice.
(chicken fried)

Waiter: I'm sorry. What kind of rice?

Customer: The chicken fried rice.

Waiter: Okay, one chicken fried rice. Anything else?

Customer:

1. In a Fast Food Place:

Two (mumble mumble) shakes
(chocolate)

2. In a Motel:

A room with a (mumble mumble) bed
(double)

3. In a Copy Store:

15 sheets of (mumble mumble) paper
(goldenrod)

4. In a Donut Shop:

4 (mumble mumble) donuts
(chocolate covered)

5. At a Gas Station:

10 gallons of (mumble mumble) gas
(super unleaded)

6. In a Restaurant:

6 tacos (mumble mumble)
(de carnitas)

7. In a Bakery:

12 (mumble mumble) croissants
(ham and cheese)

8. In a Convenience Store:

2 packs of (mumble mumble) cigarettes
(low tar Lasem)

9. In an Ice Cream Shop:

1 scoop of (mumble mumble) ice cream
(red bean)

10. In a Motel:

2 rooms with (mumble mumble) beds
(queen size)

Now make up your own examples.

1. _____

2. _____

3. _____

Part II: Repeat and Double-Check

Sometimes when employees take an order, they repeat some part of the order:

Clerk: May I help you?

Customer: I would like these shirts laundered and the pants dry cleaned.

Clerk: Okay, shirts laundered and pants dry cleaned.
Is a Wednesday pick-up okay?

Quick Practice

The customer places the order. The clerk listens and repeats.
   The clerk starts with: "What can I do for you?"
   Work in pairs and follow the example.

Clerk: What can I do for you?

Customer: I would like to have this film developed and these pictures reprinted.

Clerk: Okay, film developed and pictures reprinted. We should have your
order ready by Friday, next week.

1. At a Gas Station:
I would like my tires inflated and my oil checked.

2. At a Jewelry Store:
I would like to have this stone reset and this watch repaired.

3. To the Repairman:
I would like to have my faucet repaired and my pipes inspected.

4. To the Locksmith:
I would like to have these keys duplicated and this lock oiled.

5. To the Beautician:
I would like to have my hair set and my bangs cut.

6. At a Restaurant:
I would like my eggs over-easy and my steak rare.

Part III: Asking "How Many . . . ?"

There are different ways of double-checking information. Sometimes you hear:

Customer: Let me have three orders of chow mein and (mumble) potstickers.

Clerk: Three orders of chow mein and how many potstickers?

Customer: Eight.

Clerk: Okay, three orders of chow mein and eight potstickers. Anything else?

Quick Practice

One person will be the customer or guest; another one will be the service person.
    The customer will ask for the item; the service person will say, ". . . . . . and how many . . . . . ?" The customer will repeat the number. Work in pairs and follow the example. Only the customer looks at the text.

AT A COPY STORE:

Customer: I would like five copies on regular paper and (mumble) copies on pink paper. (15)

Clerk: That's five copies on regular paper and how many on pink paper?

Customer: Fifteen.

---

1. At a Gas Station:
10 gallons of gas and (mumble) maps of L.A. county (2)

2. In a Fast Food Restaurant:
3 cheeseburgers and (mumble) orders of chicken nuggets (5)

3. In a Mexican Take-out Restaurant:
5 burritos and (mumble) tacos (6)

4. In a Hardware Store:
1 pipe wrench and (mumble) washers (15)

5. At a Butcher's:
7 pork chops and (mumble) hot dogs (14)

6. In a Market:
6 lbs. (pounds) of tomatoes and (mumble) mangos (5)

Part IV: Asking for Clarification

Your instructor will be the customer. You will be the clerk. Listen to what your instructor says and then repeat the order. If you don't understand, ask the instructor to explain or to show you. Then double-check to make sure that you understood correctly.

Use the examples as your guide.

IN A COPY STORE:

Customer: I would like 15 copies of this text, and I'd like to have them collated and stapled.

Clerk: That's 15 — one five — right? And you want them stapled and what?

Customer: Stapled and collated.

Clerk: I'm sorry. I still don't understand. Could you show me what you mean?

Customer: You know, collated; put in order: page one, page two, page three.

Clerk: Oh, I get it. Fifteen copies, stapled and put in order. I'll get it for you right away.

Listen to your teacher read the following customer orders.

1. At a Copy Store
2. At a Donut Shop
3. In a Fast Food Place
4. In a Motel
5. At an Ice Cream Shop

6. In a Convenience Store
7. In a Repair Shop
8. In a Restaurant
9. In a Bakery
10. At a Gas Station

MAKING IT WORK

Discussion/Vocabulary

When people start working in restaurants, stores, motels, repair shops, etc., they often hear words that are new to them. After working for awhile, they get used to the special vocabulary of their jobs, and it becomes much easier to understand what customers want. Sometimes, it is possible to "guess" what a customer is saying. In such a case, it is especially important to repeat the customer's order.

What do customers ask for in donut shops, restaurants, garages, motels, gas stations, or repair service places? Make a guess and discuss your answers with others in your group. Then work together to make a vocabulary list.

1. At a Bakery or Donut Shop:

_____

_____

_____

_____

2. In a Fast Food Restaurant:

_____

_____

_____

_____

3. In a Restaurant:

_____

_____

_____

_____

4. At a Service Station:

_____

_____

_____

_____

5. At an Automotive Garage:

_____
_____
_____
_____

6. At a Copy Store:

_____
_____
_____
_____

7. In an Ice Cream Store:

_____
_____
_____
_____

8. At a Customer's House (Repair Service):

_____
_____
_____
_____

9. At a Motel:

_____
_____
_____
_____

10. At a First-Class Hotel:

_____
_____
_____
_____

Communication Skills Practice

Choose a situation. One student is the customer and the other is the clerk, waiter, or salesperson.

ROLES

Customer: Places an order

Asks questions ("Do you have . . ."
"How much . . ."
"Where is . . ."
"Where are . . .")

Employee: Takes the order
Repeats what customer wants
Gives answers

The employee starts with: "May I help you?"

---

1. At a Bakery

Customer: Orders several items from display case; orders enough for four people.

2. At a Fast Food Restaurant

🥣	VEGETABLE SOUP	$ .85	☕	COFFEE, TEA	$ .50
🍔	HAMBURGER	1.25	🥤	ORANGE JUICE, MILK	.75
🍔	CHEESEBURGER	1.50	🥧	APPLE PIE	.85
🌭	HOT DOG	1.00	🍰	CAKE	.75
🥪	CHEESE SANDWICH	1.25	🍨	ICE CREAM	.75

Customer: Orders food from picture menu; also orders drinks; orders enough food for two adults and three children.

3. At a Gas Station

Customer: Tells attendant how much gas he wants; asks for additional service (clean windshield; check air pressure in tires; check oil; add oil).

4. In a Copy Store

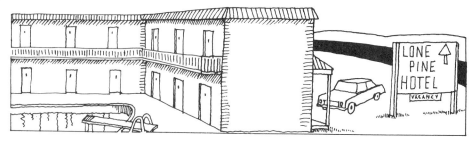

Customer: Orders fifteen copies of a magazine article; wants copies on legal size paper; wants copies stapled and collated.

5. In a Motel

Customer: Makes a reservation; chooses a room (single beds or double bed; first floor or upper floor; room in back or room overlooking pool).

6. In an Ice Cream Store

Customer: Orders several scoops of ice cream (enough for four children); orders different flavors.

7. In a Restaurant

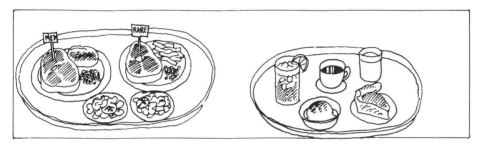

Customer: Orders steak (medium/rare/well done); orders soup or salad; orders baked potato or french fries; orders something to drink; orders dessert.

8. In a Television Repair Shop

Customer: Explains that something is wrong with the television (picture is fuzzy or there is snow on the screen; there is no sound or there is a high-pitched sound).

Clerk: Repeats the problem. Explains what he is going to do.

Moving Up Faster

Good service employees carefully listen to what customers want and then respond to the order. But successful employees do even more. They try to "anticipate" a customer's need; that is, they try to guess what the customer might want and offer him or her something "extra."

For example, these service employees may say the following:

1. In a Restaurant or Bakery:

- Would you like a salad with your meal?
- Would you care for something to drink?
- How about some dessert today?
- We have a special on donuts today: twelve for two dollars.
- Would your daughter like to see a child's menu?
- Can I bring you some ketchup or steak sauce?

2. At a Full-Service Gas Station with Car Wash:

- Do you want me to check your oil?
- Would you like to have your car washed?
- Your tires seem low. Would you like me to check them?

3. In a Store:

- How about a new tie to go with that shirt?
- Are you interested in a purse to match your shoes?
- We've got some fresh strawberries today, if you are interested.

4. In a Copy Store:

- I can put your resume on bond paper if you would like.
- Would you like to have these copies stapled and collated?

5. In a Motel or Hotel:

- We have some rooms with hair dryers and extra mirrors. Would you like one of those?
- We have free donuts and coffee in the lobby in the morning, if you'd like to come down.

Role play several situations from the Communication Skills section again and try to offer the customer something "extra."

Progress Report

Service employees need to remember many things. They should be friendly and helpful. They need to make sure that they understand what the customer wants and sometimes they should offer the customer additional items. How well did your group do in "playing" the service person? Fill out a progress report for the people you observed.

How good was the service employee? Check the appropriate box.

	DID WELL	SOME PROBLEMS	NEEDS MORE PRACTICE
1. Sounded friendly; looked customer in the eye; was helpful; smiled			
2. Repeated what customer wanted; asked questions when not sure; double-checked numbers			
3. Was easy to understand; spoke loudly and clearly enough			
4. Offered customer additional item			

Overall evaluation:

_____ Fantastic! This person is ready to go to work.

_____ Pretty good under the circumstances!

_____ Not bad. With a little practice this person will do well.

Case Studies

Case I

Discuss the following case and decide what Anton should do.

Anton has just started working in a copy store. A customer comes in and orders several copies of a paper. Anton is not sure whether the customer wants 13 or 30 copies. He asks the customer to repeat. The customer repeats the number, more loudly this time, but Anton is still not sure whether she said 30 or 13. The customer is starting to look annoyed.

What should Anton do?

_____ **1.** Anton should make thirteen copies. If the customer wants 30, he can always make more.

_____ **2.** Anton should ask the manager to talk to the customer and find out how many copies she wants.

_____ **3.** Anton should go ahead and make 30 copies. If the customer wants 13 copies, he should only charge her for 13 copies and throw out the extra copies.

_____ **4.** Other:_____

Discussion

In your opinion, which answers are good? Which answers could cause problems later on? Put a check (✓) next to the number. Discuss your opinion with others in your group. Be prepared to explain your reasons.

	GOOD	PROBLEM
1.		
2.		
3.		
4.		

Overall, what would be the best choice for Anton? Why?

_____

_____

What should Anton remember for next time?

_____

_____

Case II

Discuss the following case and decide what Kyun should do.

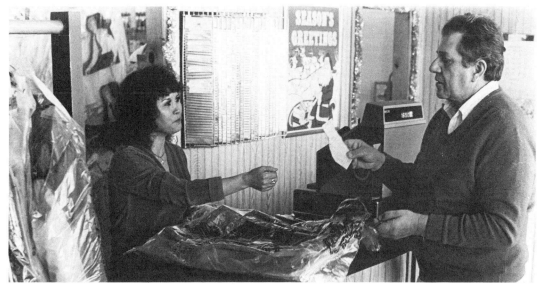

Kyun is working in a dry cleaning store that her family owns. She gets a call from a customer. The customer says, "Hi, this is Jim West. I'd like to know if my suits are ready." She says, "Just a minute, please," and walks towards the clothes racks. All of a sudden she realizes that she did not pay attention when the customer gave her his name. She feels very foolish.

What should Kyun do?

_____ **1.** Kyun should go and ask her brother to straighten things out.

_____ **2.** Kyun should get back on the phone and say, "Excuse me, how do you spell your name?"

_____ **3.** Kyun should get back on the phone and say, "I'm sorry. I didn't catch your name."

_____ **4.** Kyun should get back on the phone and say, "What is your name, sir?"

_____ **5.** Kyun should look through the names on the rack hoping one of the names will make her remember the customer's name.

_____ **6.** Other:_____

_____

Discussion

In your opinion, which is the best answer? Which is the second best, etc. In the opinion of your group, which answer is best? Which is second best, etc.

List your choices on the chart below.

	MY OPINION	GROUP'S OPINION
Best choice		
Second best choice		
Third best choice		
Next to worst choice		
Worst choice		

GETTING DOWN TO BASICS

Calculating Skills

Service employees need to be able to understand numbers *and* pronounce numbers clearly. This is especially important for prices, phone numbers, and room numbers.

Read the following numbers aloud. Follow the examples.

(714) 597-4019	seven one four — five/nine/seven — four/O/one/nine
(800) 761-4000	eight hundred — seven/six/one — four/thousand
Room 217	room two seventeen
Room 2450	room twenty-four fifty
$ 25.17	twenty-five dollars and seventeen cents or twenty-five/seventeen
$ 1.03	one dollar and three cents or one/O/three
Credit Card Exp. Dt: 08/88	Credit Card Expiration Date: eight/eighty-eight

Read the following numbers aloud and pronounce them clearly.

1. (205) 421-1373
2. Room 2716
3. (716) 420-1605
4. (890) 745-3000
5. $1.03
6. Room 2019
7. $413.30
8. $.42
9. $871.17
10. (654) 881-5534
11. Room 405
12. $7.95
13. (213) 403-7610
14. $76.10
15. Credit Card No:
    3632-383296-01006, Exp. Dt. 01/88

Reading/Scanning

Listen to the customer orders you will hear your teacher read. Then read the list
below as fast as you can and put a check (✓) next to the appropriate item.

A. In a Copy Store:

	Order A	Order B	Order C	Order D
Letter size	_____	_____	_____	_____
Legal size	_____	_____	_____	_____
11 × 17	_____	_____	_____	_____
Reductions	_____	_____	_____	_____
Enlargements	_____	_____	_____	_____
On to colored paper	_____	_____	_____	_____
On to 100% cotton	_____	_____	_____	_____
On to linen	_____	_____	_____	_____
Mailing labels	_____	_____	_____	_____
Collating	_____	_____	_____	_____
Special Handling	_____	_____	_____	_____
Stapling	_____	_____	_____	_____
Self-Service copies	_____	_____	_____	_____

Now listen to this order.

B. At a Snack Bar:

1. _____ HAMBURGER

2. _____ CHEESEBURGER

3. _____ PATTY/TUNA MELT

4. _____ GRILLED CHEESE

5. _____ GRILLED BEEF & CHEESE

6. _____ GRILLED HAM AND CHEESE

7. _____ HOT DOG/CHILI

8. _____ POLISH SAUSAGE

9. _____ CHILI/SOUP

10. _____ BARBECUED PORK

11. _____ FISH BURGER

12. _____ TACO

13. _____ BEEF AND BEAN BURRITO

14. _____ TOSTADA

15. _____ EGG-A-MUFFIN

16. _____ HAM & EGG

17. _____ EGG SANDWICH

18. _____ FRENCH FRIES

19. _____ ONION RINGS

20. _____ DELI ROAST BEEF

21. _____ SUBMARINE SANDWICH

22. _____ CHICKEN FRIED RICE

23. _____ EGGROLL

24. _____ SHRIMP FRIED RICE

25. _____ CHOW MEIN NOODLES

26. _____ ICED TEA

27. _____ COLA DRINK

28. _____ LEMONADE

29. _____ MILK

30. _____ COFFEE

31. _____ CAKE/PIE

32. _____ ICE CREAM

Writing/Spelling

Service employees often have to write down a customer's name, and then use the name later on. A service person has to be good at listening to names, writing them down, and pronouncing them correctly. The following exercise will give you practice in dealing with names. Listen to the names and write them down.

1. _____
2. _____
3. _____
4. _____
5. _____
6. _____
7. _____
8. _____
9. _____
10. _____
11. _____
12. _____
13. _____

14. _____
15. _____
16. _____
17. _____
18. _____
19. _____
20. _____
21. _____
22. _____
23. _____
24. _____
25. _____

OUT IN THE REAL WORLD

Assignment I: Learning from Experience

Do you remember an experience you had outside of school where you did not understand somebody or they did not understand you?

Tell what happened and explain the misunderstanding. Discuss whose fault it was.

_____

_____

_____

_____

_____

_____

_____

Assignment II: Learning through Observation

Many people improve their language and communication skills by paying special attention to what people around them are saying and doing. They make notes about what they see and hear and discuss their observations later with friends or teachers.

As you go shopping or eat in restaurants, watch the service employees very carefully. What do they do and say when a customer orders? Write down the place that you visited and three examples. What do service employees do if they don't understand?

1. Place_____
What did the service employee do and say?

_____

_____

_____

_____

_____

2. Place_____
What did the service employee do and say?

_____

_____

_____

_____

_____

3. Place_____
What did the service employee do and say?

_____

_____

_____

_____

_____

Chapter 2

Responding to Simple Requests for Information

"Are there any nice restaurants around here?"

OVERVIEW

Service employees often have to help customers who want information about restaurants, movies, or other forms of entertainment. Many times customers and guests will ask a question and the clerk will answer with another question.

1. At a motel, the customer may ask:
Are there any good restaurants around here?

The motel desk clerk may answer:
There are several restaurants in the area. What kind of food do you like?

2. At a convenience store, the customer may want to know:
Do you carry Lasem cigarettes?

The clerk may answer:
Yes, we do. Soft or hard pack?

INTERACTING

At the Front Desk of a Hotel

Many times guests in hotels ask for information, recommendations and directions.
You will hear two different interactions between a desk clerk and a hotel guest. Listen and decide how well each clerk handles requests for information.

Interaction I: We don't have a Chinese/Mexican restaurant around here.

What Is Your Opinion?

Circle the answer that you think is best.

1. The desk clerk is trying to be nice, but she has trouble with her English.
2. The desk clerk is doing a good job.
3. The desk clerk is not very polite, but that's okay. It's not her job to give directions to restaurants.

Discuss your answer with the other people in your group and explain your reasons.

Comprehension Questions

1. Who is talking?
2. What is the conversation about?
3. What does the guest want?
4. Does the desk clerk give good answers? Explain.
5. What is the first question the guest asks?
6. What does the desk clerk say in turn? Is that answer okay? Explain.
7. Does the desk clerk know where the Thai restaurant is?
8. What does she say? Does she offer to ask someone else?
9. Does the clerk give the guest good directions?
10. Does the desk clerk sound polite and friendly? Does she sound helpful? Explain.

Interaction II: What kind of food do you like?

Comprehension Questions

1. Would you hire desk clerk II for your hotel? Why or why not?

2. The guest asks about a restaurant. What is the desk clerk's answer?

3. Does the desk clerk understand ethnic food? What does he say?

4. Does the desk clerk know if there is a Thai restaurant in town? What does he say? What does he do?

5. What does the manager tell the desk clerk?

6. What does the desk clerk say about the Thai Palace?

7. What directions does the desk clerk give the customer? (draw a map)

8. Does the customer need a map? What does he say?

9. Does the customer sound satisfied with the help he has received? What does he say?

10. How does the desk clerk end the conversation?

Let's Compare

1. Both desk clerks say: "May I help you?"
   What is the difference?

2. The customer asks "Are there any nice restaurants near the hotel?"

   What answer does desk clerk I give? _____

   What answer does desk clerk II give? _____

3. Neither desk clerk knows what "ethnic" means.

   What does clerk I say? _____
   Does he sound friendly?

   What does clerk II say? _____
   Does the clerk sound friendly?

4. Neither desk clerk is sure if there is a Thai restaurant near the hotel.

   What does clerk I do? _____

   What does clerk II do? _____

5. Both desk clerks give directions.
   What is the difference?

6. Both customers say: "Thank you. You have been very helpful." What is the difference?

34　　**Responding to Simple Requests for Information**

Now It's Your Turn

Are There Any Nice Restaurants Around Here?

Practice the customer/clerk interaction. One student is the guest, another student is the desk clerk. A third student is the manager. Try to be polite, friendly, and helpful.

ROLES

Guest: Wants to find out where he can get something to eat.
Asks questions about different restaurants.

Desk Clerk: Finds out what kind of food customer likes.
Recommends different restaurants.
Gets information from manager if necessary.
Gives directions.
Offers to draw a map.

Manager: Gives directions to restaurant.

Role Play Checklist

Watch other students play the role of guest and desk clerk. Was the desk clerk friendly, polite and helpful? Circle *yes* or *no* and discuss your answers with the class.

1. The desk clerk offered to help the customer.   yes/no
Did he/she sound friendly?   yes/no

2. The desk clerk tried to find out what the guest likes.   yes/no

3. The desk clerk asked questions when he/she did not understand something.   yes/no
Did he/she sound polite?   yes/no

4. The desk clerk asked the manager for help.   yes/no
Did he/she explain things clearly?   yes/no

5. The desk clerk gave clear directions.   yes/no

6. The desk clerk offered to draw a map.   yes/no
Was the map clear?   yes/no

7. How did the clerk sound overall? Circle the answer that you think is best.
   a) at times friendly, at times unfriendly
   b) friendly and helpful
   c) unfriendly and rude
   d) friendly, but not very helpful

   e) _____

8. What could the clerk do better next time?

Match-Up

Sometimes service employees will answer a question with another question to find out what the customer really wants.

IN A CONVENIENCE STORE

Customer: Do you carry Lasem cigarettes?

Clerk: Soft pack or hard pack?

Customer: Hard pack.

Clerk: One-twenty, please.

AT A BOOKSTORE

Customer: Do you have the book *Megatrends?*

Clerk: Hardcover or paperback?

Customer: How much is the hardcover?

Clerk: Eighteen seventy-nine.

Customer: I'll take the paperback.

Match the customer question with the employee question. Write the letter next to the number.

CUSTOMER QUESTIONS

_____ **1.** Do you sell Kurin beer?

_____ **2.** I'm looking for a yellow turtleneck, size 7.

_____ **3.** Could I book a room for tonight for my friend and myself?

_____ **4.** How do I get to Century City from here?

_____ **5.** Could I get change for a fifty?

_____ **6.** Do you sell any alarm clocks?

_____ **7.** Could I have eggs with my pancakes?

_____ **8.** Would it be possible to get this coat cleaned by Saturday?

_____ **9.** How much are your cheeseburgers?

_____ **10.** Four people for lunch, please.

_____ **11.** I would like a glass of wine, please.

SERVICE EMPLOYEE QUESTIONS

a) Digital or regular?
b) Single or double?
c) Morning or afternoon?
d) By freeway or surface streets?
e) Red, white or rose?
f) Cotton or wool?
g) Smoking or non-smoking?
h) Sunnyside up or overeasy?
i) Bottles or cans?
j) Tens, fives, twenties?
k) Twin beds or double bed?

LEARNING THE LANGUAGE

Sometimes the best answer to a question is another question.

Part I: Asking "What Kind...?"

In Interaction II, you heard the following:

Clerk: May I help you?

Guest: Are there any nice restaurants around here?

Clerk: What kind of *food do you like?*

Guest: Ethnic food.

Clerk: Let me check with the manager. I'll be right back.

Sometimes you will hear:

Clerk: Good morning. What can I do for you?

Customer: Do you have heavy-duty tires?

Clerk: What kind of *car do you drive?*

Customer: A Monota.

Clerk: Let me see what I can find out.

Quick Practice

One person will be the customer or guest, another the service person. The customer asks for information or makes a request. The clerk asks "What kind.........?" and then gives an answer. Work in pairs and follow the examples.

Clerk: May I help you?

Customer: Are there any good movies playing around here?

Clerk: What kind of movies do you like?

Customer: Adventure movies.

Clerk: I think *Rambo*'s playing at the mall.

Customer:	Could you send a service person to my home? My refrigerator is broken.
Repair Service Manager:	What kind of refrigerator do you have?
Customer:	A *C.J. Neppy*'s.
Repair Service Manager:	Okay. We'll send a man out on Wednesday.

1. Customer: Could you show me your watches?

Clerk: _____
(watch/looking for)

Customer: _____

Clerk: _____

2. Customer: Could I have a scoop of ice cream?

Clerk: _____
(cone/would you like)

Customer: _____

Clerk: _____

3. Customer: Could I have a salad with my hamburger?

Waitress/ Waiter: _____
(dressing/would you like)

Customer: _____

Waitress/ Waiter: _____

4. Customer: Could you add some oil to the engine?

Attendant: _____
(oil/need)

Customer: _____

5. *Customer:* Could you make ten copies of this letter?

Clerk: _____
(paper/want)

Customer: _____

Clerk: _____

6. *Customer:* Does your store carry pet food?

Clerk: _____
(pet/have)

Customer: _____

Clerk: _____

7. *Customer:* I'm looking for a black dress.

Clerk: _____
(material/have in mind)

Customer: _____

Clerk: _____

On Your Own

1. *Customer:* Could you recommend a nice restaurant?

Clerk: _____

Customer: _____

Clerk: _____

2. *Customer:* Do you sell windshield wipers?

Clerk: _____

Customer: _____

Clerk: _____

3. *Customer:* Can you recommend something I can read on the bus to New York?

Clerk: _____

Customer: _____

Clerk: _____

Part II: Giving Directions

Service employees often have to give directions.

In Interaction II, you heard the following.

Clerk: There's a Thai restaurant in the shopping center on Main Street.

Customer: How do I get to Main Street?

Clerk: Do you see the street out here? That's Pioneer. You take that to the first light. That's Main Street. You make a right on Main Street and the shopping center is about half a block down on your right. You can't miss it.

Sometimes you will hear:

Customer: Could you tell me where the nearest mailbox is?

Clerk: Just go out that door and turn right. It's about half a block down on the other side of the street in front of the drugstore.

Quick Practice

One person will make a request for information, another person will give directions. A third person will help to give directions if the service employee is not sure. (Use information from the neighborhood around your school or training site.)

    The customer will start with: "Excuse me . . . . ." Follow the example.
    The customer will repeat the instructions.

Customer: Excuse me, do you know where I can buy some aspirin?

Employee: I think there's a drugstore close by. Let me check with the manager to make sure.

Employee to Manager: Where's the drugstore?

Manager: Two blocks down, behind Frank's.

Employee to Customer: Make a right out of the parking lot, follow the street. It's two blocks down behind Frank's Supermarket, on the left.

Customer: Okay. Right out here, then two blocks down on the left. Thanks.

---

1. Excuse me, could you direct me to the nearest gas station?

Employee: _____

_____

2. I'm looking for the shopping center.

Employee: _____

_____

3. Could you tell me where the nearest pay phone is?

Employee: _____

_____

4. Is there a place where we can get some ice cream for the kids?

Employee: _____

_____

5. Where can I buy some cigarettes?

Employee: _____

_____

6. How do I get to the freeway (expressway) from here?

Employee: _____

_____

7. Can you tell me where the nearest bus stop is?

Employee: _____

_____

8. I need to make a phone call. Where's a pay phone?

Employee: _____

_____

9. I'd like to get these pictures developed. Where can I take them?

Employee: _____

_____

10. The heel on my shoe came off. Where could I get that repaired?

Employee: _____

_____

11. I need to make some copies of these papers. Where can I go?

Employee: _____

_____

12. Where could I get this watch repaired?

Employee: _____

_____

13. I'm looking for the bathrooms.

Employee: _____

_____

14. Is there a place where I can buy a city map?

Employee: _____

_____

15. I'd like to get a nice meal. What restaurant do you recommend?

Employee: _____

_____

16. Where can I buy concert tickets?

Employee: _____

_____

17. I think my battery is low. Where can I get it recharged?

Employee: _____

_____

18. I just lost a filling in my tooth. Is there a dentist close by?

Employee: _____

_____

19. Where can I get a quick cup of coffee?

Employee: _____

_____

20. I lost my green card. Where's the Department of Immigration and Naturalization?

Employee: _____

_____

MAKING IT WORK

Discussion/Vocabulary

In the United States, customers have many choices. For example, when a customer eats dinner or lunch in a coffee shop, he/she may have a choice between soup or salad, or between baked potatoes and french fries with the meal.

Good employees ask questions and let customers know what choices are available.

AT A COFFEE SHOP:
- Would you like soup or salad with your lunch?
- What kind of dressing do you want on your salad?
- How do you want your hamburger cooked? Rare, medium, or well-done?
- Would you like steak sauce with your hamburger?
- Would you like french fries or potato salad with your hamburger?
- Would you like ketchup with your french fries?
- What would you like to drink?
- Do you take milk and sugar in your coffee?
- Would you care for any dessert?
- Would you like whipped cream or ice cream with your pie?
- Would you like to take the rest of the pie home with you?

What other questions could a service employee ask? What choices could he or she give the customer?

1. In an Ethnic Restaurant:
   (Mexican, Vietnamese, Arabic, Portuguese, Yugoslavian, etc. Choose one.)

_____

_____

_____

_____

2. At a Dry Cleaner's:

_____

_____

_____

_____

3. At a Gas Station:

_____

_____

_____

_____

4. At a Copy Store:

_____

_____

_____

_____

5. In a Hotel:

_____

_____

_____

_____

6. At an Automotive Garage:

_____

_____

_____

_____

7. At a Fancy Restaurant:

_____

_____

_____

_____

Communication Skills Practice

Choose a situation. One student is the customer, the other is the clerk, waiter or salesperson.

ROLES

Customer: Places an order.
Asks questions: ("Do you have . . . . ?")
("Can I get . . . . ?")

Employee: Asks questions to find out what customer wants.
Explains choices available.
Takes the order and repeats the order.

The employee will start with: "May I help you?"

1. In a Restaurant

Customer: Orders a steak dinner in a restaurant

Waiter finds out: Would customer like soup or salad?
(if soup, what kind of soup:
clam chowder or chicken noodle
if salad, what kind of dressing:
Blue Cheese, French, or Italian?)

How would customer like his/her steak cooked (rare/medium/well-done)?

Would customer like mashed potatoes, baked potatoes, or french fries?
(if baked potatoes, with butter or sour cream?)

Would customer care for dessert?

What would customer like to drink?
(beer, wine (red, white), soft drinks)

2. At a Copy Store

Customer: Wants to have a five page letter copied.

Copy clerk finds out: How many copies would customer like?

Does customer want pages collated (put in order)?

Does customer want pages stapled?

When does customer want to pick up the copies?

3. At a Dry Cleaner's

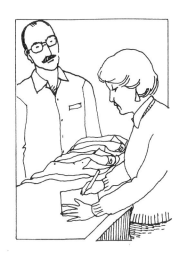

Customer: Wants to have one suit and two shirts cleaned

Dry cleaner finds out: Does customer want shirts dry cleaned or laundered (washed)? (Laundered is cheaper.)

Does customer want missing buttons replaced?

Is Saturday pick up okay?

4. At a Motel Desk

Guest: Wants a room

Desk Clerk finds out: Does customer have a reservation? When would customer like the room?

How long will guest be staying? How many people will be staying in the room?

Would guest like single bed or double bed?

5. At an Ethnic Restaurant

Customer: Orders the Lunch Special

Counter Clerk finds out: Would customer like pork, shrimp, or beef?

Would customer like steamed rice or fried rice with the order?

What would customer like to drink?

Would customer like chopsticks or a fork?

6. At an Ice Cream Store

Customer: Wants to buy some ice cream
Finds out what flavors are available
("What flavors do you have?")

Chooses ice cream and topping

Clerk finds out: What flavor does customer want? (available flavors: vanilla, strawberry, boysenberry, peach, chocolate chip)

How many scoops does customer want?

Does customer want ice cream in a bowl or on a cone?
(if cone, sugar cone or regular;
if bowl, what topping does customer want: nuts, chocolate sauce, whipped cream)

7. At a Jewelry Store

Customer: Wants to buy digital watch with alarm
Doesn't want to spend more than $75

Compares price and value of two watches

Sales Clerk: Finds out what customer wants and then makes suggestions

Points out that Watch B has alarm, stopwatch, and is waterproof

Talks about advantages of Watch B
Tries to sell Watch B

Moving Up Faster

Good clerks do more than just answer questions, they try to be good salespeople, too. Experienced salespeople try to make suggestions and explain special sales.

For example, an experienced salesperson might say the following:

At a Full Service Gas Station and Car Wash:

- Would you like super unleaded gas?
- Would you like for me to check the oil?
- Should I look under the hood?
- How about a car wash today?
- How about a wax to go with the wash? We're having a half-price sale this week only.
- Cash or credit card? You get a discount on cash.

At a Hotel:

- We now have rooms with jacuzzis. Would you be interested?
- We offer a special weekend rate if you'd like to stay until Sunday.
- We have a very nice restaurant in the hotel if you would like to eat dinner close by.
- We have secretarial services available if you need typing done.

At a Clothing Store:

- Can I help you choose a tie to go with that shirt?
- How about a skirt to go with that blouse?
- We have some scarves on sale that would look great with that dress.

Choose one situation in a hotel, restaurant, gas station or clothing store. Role-play the situation and act like an experienced salesperson.

Progress Report

To be effective, service employees need to remember many things. They should be friendly and helpful. They need to make sure that they understand what the customer wants; and if appropriate, they should offer the customer additional items. How well did your group do in "playing" the service person? Fill out a progress report for the people you observed.

What did the service employee do? Check the appropriate box.

	DID WELL	SOME PROBLEMS	NEEDS MORE PRACTICE
1. Used a friendly tone; looked customer in the eye; appeared helpful; smiled			
2. Asked questions to find out what customer wants; offered choices; gave explanations			
3. Was easy to understand; spoke loudly and clearly			
4. Offered customer additional item; explained sales items			

Overall evaluation:

_____ Fantastic! This person is ready to go to work.

_____ Pretty good under the circumstances!

_____ Not bad. With a little practice this person will do well.

Case Study

Discuss the following case and decide what Pat should do.

Pat is a waiter in a small restaurant. One day a customer orders salad. Pat says: "What kind of dressing would you like?" The customer answers: "Ranch style, please." The restaurant has only French, Thousand Island, and oil and vinegar dressing. What should Pat do?

_____ **1.** Pat should say: "What IS Ranch Style? I've never even heard of it."

_____ **2.** Pat should say: "I'm sorry. We only have French, Thousand Island, and vinegar and oil."

_____ **3.** Pat should just bring the customer Thousand Island dressing; most customers like it.

_____ **4.** Pat should say: "I'm sorry. We don't have Ranch Style dressing."

_____ **5.** Other: _____

_____

Discussion

In your opinion, which answers are good? Which answers could cause problems later on? Put a check (✔) next to the number. Discuss your opinion with others in your group. Be prepared to explain your reasons to the class.

	GOOD	PROBLEM
1.		
2.		
3.		
4.		

Overall, what would be the best choice for Pat? Why?

_____

_____

_____

What should Pat remember for next time?

_____

_____

_____

GETTING DOWN TO BASICS

Reading and Calculating: "How Much Do I Owe You?"

Service employees often have to add up prices and make change. Some establishments have adding machines, but in other places employees may have to add numbers themselves.

With a partner choose one situation: at a copy store, a dry cleaner's, a restaurant or a convenience store. The customer decides how much money he wants to spend. He tells the clerk/waiter what he wants. The clerk/waiter writes up a bill. Use the price list on page 53.

1. At a Convenience Store

$ _____

$ _____

$ _____

$ _____

_____

2. At a Dry Cleaner's

$ _____

$ _____

$ _____

$ _____

_____

3. At a Restaurant

$ _____

$ _____

$ _____

$ _____

_____

4. At a Copy Store

$ _____

$ _____

$ _____

$ _____

_____

Price List

CONVENIENCE STORE

Milk (1 quart)	.79
Soft drinks (cans)	.60
Soda (2 liter bottle)	2.05
Instant coffee (4 oz. jar)	4.49
Bag of potato chips	1.30
TV Guide	.60
People Magazine	1.50

DRY CLEANER'S

Pants	2.50
Dress	4.00
Sportscoat	6.00
Sweater	3.50
Laundered Shirt	1.25
2-Piece Suit	7.50
Replace missing button	.75

COPY STORE

White

Letter Size	4½ cents
Legal Size	5½ cents

Colored
(Blue, pink, yellow)

Letter Size	6 cents
Legal Size	7 cents

Multiple Copies
(White)

100	4.50
200	7.00
500	14.50

Special Services

Collating (per copy)	½ cent
Stapling	2 cents

RESTAURANT

Steak Dinner	9.95
Fish Dinner	6.80
Hamburger	2.25
French fries	1.25
Salad	1.00
Cola	.60
Milk	.65
Carrot cake	1.40
Hamburger	3.50
Enchiladas	3.75
Tacos	2.50
Submarine	2.75

Writing

Usually, a customer gets a receipt each time he pays for a product or a service. Often a cash register receipt is enough, but sometimes the employee has to make out a hand-written receipt.

　　With a partner, choose a situation: at a copy store, a dry cleaner's, a restaurant or a convenience store. The customer orders some items and then asks for a hand-written receipt. The employee writes the receipt. Use the price list on page 53.

QUANTITY	NAME OF ITEM	PRICE/ITEM	TOTAL
2 six packs	Cool Cola	$3.25 each	$6.50
3 bags	Lies Potato Chips	$1.75 each	$5.25

1. At a Dry Cleaner's:

QUANTITY	NAME OF ITEM	PRICE/ITEM	TOTAL

TOTAL :_____

2. At a Restaurant:

QUANTITY	NAME OF ITEM	PRICE/ITEM	TOTAL

TOTAL :_____

3. At a Copy Store:

QUANTITY	NAME OF ITEM	PRICE/ITEM	TOTAL

TOTAL :_____

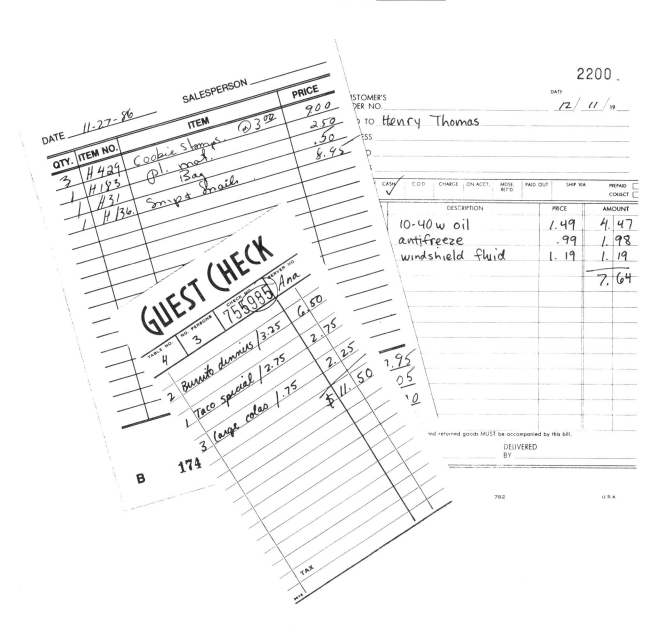

OUT IN THE REAL WORLD

Assignment I: Learning through Experience

Have you ever ordered food in a restaurant, asked for items in a store, or explained a problem to a repair person? Think about such a case and then write a dialogue about your own experience.

Assignment II: Practicing with Friends

a) Do you know how to give directions to other people? Explain to your friends in class how they can get to your house from your school or training site. Draw a map.

b) Do you sometimes wonder what movies to see, what restaurants to go to or where to get your car repaired?

Ask your friends to recommend several of the following. Ask for directions where appropriate.

1. a movie
2. a book
3. a restaurant
4. a good car repair person

5. a fast food place
6. a low-priced department store
7. a place to buy a watch
8. a nice motel

Assignment III: Learning through Observation

One of the best ways to prepare for a job is to watch people at work. Many successful employees have learned the "tricks" of working by watching other people.

Go into stores, shops, and restaurants and watch what real clerks, salespeople, waiters and waitresses say and do. Then be a customer yourself and pay attention to the clerk. Do you think he or she was friendly and helpful? Tell the class what you found out.

1. At a Restaurant

   Go to a (fast food) restaurant. Watch the customers. Watch the clerks. Then order something yourself.

   REPORT

   What did the customers say?

   _____

   _____

   _____

   What questions did the clerk ask?

   _____

   _____

   _____

   _____

   Did the clerk/waiter seem friendly and helpful? _____

   What did he or she do special? _____

   _____

2. At a Copy Store

   Take a letter or a form to a copy store. Ask to get three copies on colored paper. Ask the clerk what colors are available.

   REPORT

   What did you ask the clerk? _____

   _____

   What did the clerk say to you? _____

   _____

3. At a _____

Choose one other place to go to and observe customers and clerks. Pay attention to what people are saying and doing. Also pay attention to what tone people are using. Report back to the class.

REPORT

What did the customers say? _____

_____

_____

What did the clerk ask? _____

_____

_____

Did all the clerks sound friendly? _____

How about the customers? _____

Chapter
3
Dealing With Mistakes

"I only wanted
five dollars
worth of gas.
You gave me six."

OVERVIEW

Sometimes employees make mistakes and customers get upset. Good employees know what to say and do when they make a mistake.

1. You gave me apple pie. I wanted cherry.

I'm really sorry. I'll get you the cherry.

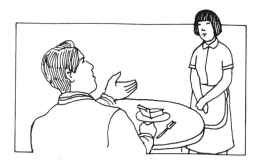

2. I asked you to bring me some hair spray. You brought me shampoo.

I'm terribly sorry. I misunderstood.
I will bring the hair spray right away.

3. I wanted a receipt. You didn't give me one.

I'm sorry. I forgot. It has been a long day.
Just a second, and I will give it to you.

INTERACTING

At a Self-Service Gas Station

Everybody makes mistakes sometimes. Experienced service employees know what to do and say when this happens. You will hear two different interactions between a gas station attendant and a customer. Listen and decide which attendant does a better job.

Interaction I: You must pay for the gas, sir.

What is Your Opinion?

Did the cashier do a good job? Circle the answer that you think is best.

1. The cashier made several mistakes. He should sound more friendly and apologize more.

2. Mistakes happen; the cashier did a good job.

3. The customer didn't explain things right. The mistake was not the cashier's fault.

4. Other:_____

_____

Discuss your answer with the other people in your group and explain your reasons.

Comprehension Questions

1. Where does the interaction take place?
2. Who is talking?
3. What does the customer want?
4. What is the first problem?
5. How does the cashier respond? What does he say?
6. What is the second problem?
7. How does the cashier respond this time? What does he say? How does he say it? (friendly?/rude?)
8. The customer explains the problem one more time. What does he say?
9. How does the cashier respond this time? What does he say?
10. The customer gets very angry. Why?
11. Who made mistakes, the customer or the cashier? Explain your reasons.
12. Did the cashier do a good job? Explain your reasons.

Interaction II: I'm really sorry. I misunderstood.

Comprehension Questions

1. What does the customer want?
2. What is the problem at the gas pump?
3. What does the cashier say when the customer explains the problem?
4. What is the second problem the customer has? What happened?
5. What does the cashier say? What explanation does he give?
6. The cashier says "I'm sorry" again. What else does he say?
7. How much money did the customer give the cashier?
8. Why does the customer need the five dollars?
9. What is the cashier's answer?
10. In your opinion, what will the customer say next?

Let's Compare

1. What is the biggest difference between the two cashiers?

   How does cashier I act?_____

   How does cashier II act?_____

2. Both cashiers made a mistake.

   What is the mistake?_____

3. The cashiers handle the mistakes differently.

   What does cashier I do and say?_____

   What does cashier II do and say?_____

4. Both cashiers apologize when the meter does not stop.

   What does cashier I say?_____

   What does cashier II say?_____

5. Both cashiers explain that the manager is not available.

   What does cashier I say?_____

   What does cashier II say?_____

6. If you were the boss, what would you tell cashier I?_____

   _____

   What would you tell cashier II?_____

   _____

Now It's Your Turn

I Only Wanted Five Dollars Worth of Gas. You Gave Me Six.

Practice the customer/gas station attendant interaction. One student is the customer, the other student is the attendant. The attendant tries to be friendly but firm.

ROLES

Customer:	Gives attendant $10.00
	Wants $5.00 worth of gas
	Explains that attendant made a mistake
	Wants his money back after the attendant gives him/her too much gas
	Gets upset
	Wants to talk to manager
Gas Station Attendant:	Punches in $10.00 worth of gas instead of $5.00
	Listens to customer
	Apologizes for mistake
	Explains what happened
	Explains why he can't give customer any money back
	Explains why manager is not available
	Explains what customer can do next

Role Play Checklist

Watch other students play the role of the customer and the gas station attendant. Was the attendant friendly or firm? Circle *Yes* or *No* and discuss your answers with the class.

1. The attendant apologized for the mistake.   yes/no
Did he/she sound sorry?   yes/no

2. The attendant explained how the mistake happened.   yes/no

3. The attendant explained why he/she could not give the customer any money back.   yes/no

4. The attendant explained why the manager was not available.   yes/no
Did he/she sound sorry?   yes/no

5. The attendant explained what the customer could do next.   yes/no
Did he/she sound friendly?   yes/no

6. How did the attendant sound overall? Circle the answer you think is best.

     a) Sounded sorry he/she made a mistake but stayed firm.

     b) Was angry and rude and blamed the customer.

     c) Was too nice; made promises he/she could not keep.

7. What could the clerk do better next time?

Match-Up

When service employees make a mistake, they often explain what they will do next.

AT AN AUTO REPAIR SHOP
Mechanic: I had told you that your car would be ready this afternoon. I'm sorry, but it took us longer than expected. We will have it ready for you by tomorrow noon.

AT A MEXICAN RESTAURANT
Waiter: You wanted rice only, no beans, didn't you? Please let me get you a new plate from the kitchen right away.

Match employee mistakes with the appropriate explanation, promise or offer.

EMPLOYEE MISTAKE

_____ **1.** I am sorry. I forgot to add the coffee to your bill.

_____ **2.** I'm sorry. I quoted you the wrong price for the hotel room.

_____ **3.** Excuse me. I think I just gave you the wrong directions to the drugstore.

_____ **4.** I'm sorry. I misunderstood. I thought you wanted regular towels.

_____ **5.** I'm sorry. I think I overcharged you on those cigarettes.

_____ **6.** I'm sorry. I must have misunderstood. I thought you said you wanted 30 copies.

_____ **7.** I'm so sorry. I didn't realize you were still eating.

_____ **8.** I'm sorry. I brought you a regular beer by mistake.

EMPLOYEE EXPLANATIONS

a) I'll only charge you for the 13.
b) I'll be right back with the beach towels.
c) Let me get you a "light" right away.
d) I'll need to take the check back so I can add it on. I'm sorry.
e) Let me deduct seven cents here.
f) You should turn right on South Street instead of left. I'm sorry. I got turned around.
g) Unfortunately the real price is $80 a night.
h) Please take your time.

LEARNING THE LANGUAGE

Making a mistake can be embarrassing, but experienced employees know what to say when mistakes happen.

Part I: Apologizing for a Mistake

In Interaction II, you heard the following:

Customer: I'm not getting any gas on Number 7. Did you turn it on?

Cashier: I'm sorry. I turned on the wrong pump. Let me try again. There. It's ready to go now.

You also heard:

Customer: I told you to give me five dollars worth of gas, but the meter didn't stop.

Cashier: I'm sorry, that was my mistake. I thought you wanted 10 dollars worth.

When service people make a mistake, they usually apologize.

They may say:
    "I'm sorry" or "I apologize."

Sometimes they also say:
    "I made a mistake" or "That was my fault."

Sometimes they explain how the mistake happened. They may say:
    "I misunderstood. I thought you . . ."

Often they explain what they are going to do next. They may say:
    "I'll do it again" or "Let me get the manager."

Quick Practice

Look at the following mistakes. Play the role of the service person. In each case apologize and explain how the mistake happened. In some cases, you need to explain what you will do next. Follow the example.

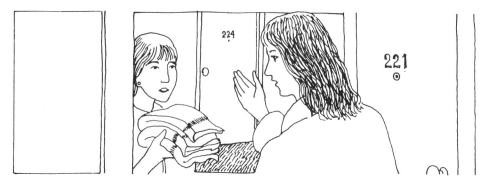

AT A HOTEL:

You are a maid in a hotel. The guest asks you to bring her two face cloths. You think she means face towels. When the guest points out your mistake . . .

You say: I'm sorry, I misunderstood. I thought you meant face towels. I'll get you two face cloths right away.

---

1. You work in a copy store. The customer wants fifty copies of a form. You make fifteen copies instead. When you realize your mistake . . .

You say:_____ , I_____.

I thought_____.

I'll_____.

2. You are a waitress in a coffee shop. You think the customer is finished, so you take her plate away. The customer says, "I'm still eating."

You say:_____ , I_____.

I thought_____.
Please take your time.

3. You work at a gas station. A customer tells you to give her five dollars worth of gas. You think she wants a fill-up. When the customer says, "What are you doing?" . . .

You say:_____ , I_____.

I thought_____.
I am really sorry.

4. You work in a fast food restaurant. The customer orders a shake. You think he wants chocolate. The customer wanted strawberry. When the customer complains. . .

You say:_____, I_____.

I thought_____.

I'll_____.

5. You work as a maid in a hotel. The guest asks you to bring him two beach towels. You think he wants bath towels. When the customer points out your mistake. . .

You say:_____, I_____.

I thought_____.

I'll_____.

Part II: Asking for Advice Before Mistakes Happen

Everybody makes mistakes. Managers and supervisors don't expect their employees to be perfect. Very often new employees ask managers or co-workers for advice to avoid mistakes.

An employee in a dry cleaner's may ask her boss:
What do I tell a customer if her clothes don't come clean?

Or, she may ask a co-worker:
What should I do if I tell a customer that his shirts will be ready and they're not?

Quick Practice

Imagine the following situations and ask what you should do. Follow the example.

AT A RESTAURANT
A customer orders a drink, but you forget to put it on the bill.

You ask the manager or other waiter or waitress:
If a customer orders a drink and I forget to put it on the bill, what should I do?

---

1. At a Hotel:
You can't find a reservation.

You ask the manager or another desk clerk:

_____

_____

2. At a Restaurant:
  a) You spill hot coffee on a customer.

    You ask the manager or another waiter or waitress:

_____

_____

  b) You drop a tray of food.

    You ask the manager or another waiter or waitress:

_____

_____

3. At a Motel:
  a) When cleaning up a room, you break a guest's glasses.

    You ask the manager or another maid:

_____

_____

  b) You accidentally place a wake-up call to the wrong room.

    You ask the manager or another operator:

_____

_____

  c) A guest asked you to wake her up with a wake-up call but you completely forgot.

    You ask the manager or another clerk:

_____

_____

4. At a Coffee Shop:

    a) You bring a customer his eggs sunny-side up instead of "over easy."

    You ask the manager or another waiter or waitress:

_____

_____

    b) A customer asks you for some ketchup, but you forget to bring it. (You remember when the customer has finished eating.)

    You ask the manager or another waiter or waitress.

_____

_____

5. At a Copy Store:
You forget to collate and staple a customer's order.

    You ask the manager or another clerk:

_____

_____

6. At a Store:

    a) You realize you forgot to charge the customer the sales tax.

    You ask the manager or another sales clerk:

_____

_____

    b) You gave a customer the wrong change.

    You ask the manager or another sales clerk:

_____

_____

7. At a Fast Food Restaurant:
You give the customer an order of french fries. The customer did not order french fries and did not pay for french fries.

    You ask the manager or another counter clerk:

_____

_____

MAKING IT WORK

Discussion/Vocabulary

Everybody makes mistakes. Some mistakes are serious (giving a customer a regular cola instead of diet cola if the customer is not allowed to eat sugar). Some mistakes are not so serious (mixing up orders at the same table). What mistakes do you think fast food clerks, waiters, parking lot attendants, copy clerks or gas station attendants might make?

Make a guess and discuss your answers with others in your group. Then make a list. In each case decide if the mistake is serious or not so serious.

1. Mistakes at a Fast Food Counter

Serious   *Not so serious*

_____   _____

_____   _____

_____   _____

2. Mistakes at a Parking Lot

Serious   *Not so serious*

_____   _____

_____   _____

_____   _____

3. Mistakes at a Hotel

Serious   *Not so serious*

_____   _____

_____   _____

_____   _____

4. Mistakes at a Convenience Store

Serious   *Not so serious*

_____   _____

_____   _____

_____   _____

5. Mistakes at a Full-Service Gas Station

Serious   *Not so serious*

_____   _____

_____   _____

_____   _____

Communication Skills Practice

Choose a situation. One student is the customer and another is the clerk, waiter, or salesperson.

ROLES

Customer: Explains what happened

Employee: Says "I'm sorry"
Gives explanation, if possible
Explains what he/she will do next

The employee starts with: "May I help you?" or "What can I do for you?"

1. At the Fast Food Counter

Customer explains: Ordered onion rings but got french fries instead.

Counter clerk: Apologizes.
Explains that he will get onion rings right away.

2. At a Parking Lot

Customer explains: Was at the parking lot a few minutes ago.
Asked the attendant for a receipt.

The attendant forgot to give a receipt.

Attendant: Apologizes.
Asks customer how much she paid.

Hands the customer the receipt.
("Here you are.")

3. At a Hotel

Customer explains: The maid brought her shampoo, but she had asked for hair spray.

Maid: Apologizes and explains what she will do.

4. At a Convenience Store

Customer explains: Was at the store earlier.
Bought cigarettes and asked for matches, but clerk forgot to give him matches.

Clerk: Apologizes.
Explains that it has been a long day.
Hands customer the matches.

5. At a Full-Service Gas Station

Customer explains: Was at the station a few minutes ago.
Just noticed that the gas cap was missing.

Attendant: Apologizes.
Explains that it was his mistake.
Says that he will get the gas cap from the office.

6. At a Copy Store

Customer explains: Wanted fifty copies but the clerk only made fifteen.

Copy clerk: Apologizes.
Explains that he misunderstood.
("I thought. . .")
Explains what he is going to do.

7. At a Fast Food Restaurant

Customer explains: Ordered a chicken taco but got a beef taco.

Waitress: Apologizes.
Explains what she is going to do.

Moving Up Faster

Employees who work hard, communicate well, think on their feet, and are able to make good decisions can become managers. Look at the following situations and decide what should be done.

1. In a Fast Food Restaurant
The counter person gives a customer the bacon burger instead of the avocado burger. The customer has started eating.

Waitress: Asks manager what she should do.

Manager: Makes a decision.

2. At a Gas Station
The attendant filled up a car with premium unleaded gas. The customer did not ask for premium.

Attendant: Explains the situation to the manager.

Manager: Makes a decision.

3. At a Customer's Home
The repair person installed a garbage disposal. The customer calls the office and says that the disposal was not properly installed. It leaks.

Repair person: Explains problem to the manager.

Manager: Makes a decision.

4. At a Copy Store
The customer calls to say that she asked the store to copy a 50-page text. Some pages are missing from the original text.

Copy Clerk: Explains problem to the manager.

Managers: Makes a decision.

5. At a Dry Cleaner's
The customer says that his clothes were supposed to be ready. They are not.

Dry Cleaner: Explains the problem to the manager.

Manager: Makes a decision.

6. In a Parking Lot
The valet parking cars scratched a customer's car.

Valet: Explains the problem to the manager.

Manager: Makes a decision.

Progress Report

When mistakes occur, service employees need to remember many things. They should apologize, give reasons why a mistake happened, and explain what they will do next. If they are not sure what to do, service employees should report the mistake to the supervisor. Serious mistakes always have to be reported. How well did your group do in handling mistakes? Fill out a progress report for the people you observed.

What did the service employee do? Check the appropriate box.

	DID WELL	SOME PROBLEMS	NEEDS MORE PRACTICE
1. Used a friendly tone; looked customer in the eye; apologized for mistake			
2. Explained reason, where necessary; explained what he/she would do next			
3. Was easy to understand; spoke loudly and clearly			
4. Asked for help or reported serious mistake to supervisor			

Overall evaluation:

_____ Fantastic! This person is ready to go to work.

_____ Pretty good under the circumstances!

_____ Not bad. With a little practice this person will do well.

Case Studies

Case I

Discuss the following case and decide what you would do in this situation.

You are working in a Chinese restaurant. A customer orders the pork fried rice and a diet cola. You bring her her lunch and the cola. When you get back to the kitchen, you realize that you made a mistake. You gave the customer a regular cola instead of a diet cola. The customer does not notice and has started drinking the cola. How would you handle the mistake?

_____ **1.** You would say nothing. Maybe the customer won't know the difference. Besides, it would be too embarrassing to say that you made a mistake.

_____ **2.** You would go to the customer's table and say: "Is everything all right?" If the customer does not mention (talk about) the cola, you don't mention (talk about) the cola.

_____ **3.** You would go to the customer, apologize and explain that you made a mistake. You offer to get the customer the diet cola.

_____ **4.** You would ask the manager to please go to the customer and explain to her that you made a mistake with the cola.

_____ **5.** Other:_____

Discussion

In your opinion, which is the best answer? Which is the second best, etc.
In the opinion of your group, which answer is best? Which is second best, etc.
List your choices in the chart below by writing down the number.

	MY OPINION	GROUP'S OPINION
Best choice:		
Second best choice:		
Third best choice:		
Next to worst choice:		
Worst choice:		

Case II

Discuss the following case and decide what Ali should do.

This is Ali's first job at a gas station. Ali gives a customer gas and takes his credit card. The customer signs the credit card slip and drives off. After the customer leaves, Ali notices that he still has the customer's credit card.
    What should Ali do?

_____ **1.** Ali should throw away the credit card. That way no one will find out about his mistake.

_____ **2.** Ali should look in the phone book to see if the customer's name is listed. If it is, he should call the customer.

_____ **3.** Ali should wait. The customer may come back in a week or so.

_____ **4.** Ali should ask another attendant what to do.

_____ **5.** Other:_____

Discussion

In your opinion, which answers are good? Which answers could cause problems later on? Put a (✔) next to the number. Discuss your opinion with others in your group. Be prepared to explain your reasons.

	GOOD	PROBLEM
1.		
2.		
3.		
4.		

What would be the best way for Ali to handle the situation?

_____

What should Ali remember for next time?_____

_____

GETTING DOWN TO BASICS

Listening Skills

Many times mistakes happen because the employee misunderstands a number or mispronounces a number so that other people become confused. To avoid such mistakes, it is important to feel comfortable with telephone numbers, prices, and room numbers.

Write down the numbers you hear.

Phone numbers	Room numbers	Prices
(213) 402-7519	2066	$20.49

Reading

Usually, public contact employees are trained by their employers. Training shows them how to do things right so that mistakes don't happen. Well, sometimes mistakes happen anyway.

When this happens, employers often leave messages to remind their employees how things should be done. The memo (message) below talks about the right way to make change. Study it and discuss what it means.

To: All Employees

From: The Management

Lately there have been a number of mistakes in the way change has been handled. Here is a reminder on proper procedures:

1. If the customer gives you the correct amount, count the money while the customer is watching. If the customer gives you the incorrect amount, repeat the exact amount the customer has to pay.

2. If the customer gives you a bill larger than the amount due, put the bill above the till of the register; do not put it into the till until you have made change. Be sure to repeat the amount due as well as the denomination of the bill you were given (Example: "That's six seventy-five [amount due] out of twenty," [denomination of customer's bill]).

3. When you give the customer back his change, indicate how much money he is receiving (Example: "Thirteen twenty-five is your change").

4. If the customer tells you that you have made a mistake, first double-check the bill you received, then recount the change you are handing back. If there are any disagreements, call the manager.

We expect everyone to follow these procedures so that mistakes involving change will be minimized.

The Management

Comprehension Questions

1. Who is the memo for?

2. Who is sending the memo?

3. Why was the memo sent?

4. What does "proper procedures" mean?

5. What should the cashier do if the customer has the correct amount?

6. What should the cashier do if the customer hands her an incorrect amount?

7. What should the cashier do if the customer hands the cashier a large bill?

8. What does "amount due" mean? Give examples.

9. What does "denomination" mean? Give examples.

10. a) What should the cashier say if the bill is three twenty-five and the customer hands her $20?

b) What should the cashier say when she hands back the change?

11. What should the cashier do when the customer says: "You've made a mistake"?

12. What will happen if everyone follows the procedures?

Writing

You are the cashier in a gas station. One afternoon, a customer asks for 5 dollars worth of gas. He gives you 5 dollars. You make a mistake and set the machine at 10 dollars. The gas pump pumps 8 dollars worth of gas into the customer's car. The customer says he does not have any money and refuses to pay the extra three dollars.

The manager, Ms. Garcia, is at a meeting and will not be back until after your shift. Leave her a note explaining what happened.

Date:_____

To:_____

From:_____

re: Cash Mistake

_____

_____

_____

_____

_____

_____

_____

_____

_____

_____

_____

_____

_____

_____

OUT IN THE REAL WORLD

Assignment I: Learning from Experience

Have you or your friends ever seen a salesperson, a clerk or an attendant make a mistake? Tell what happened and explain the mistake in detail. Explain what the employee did and how the employee tried to fix the mistake.

Assignment II: Learning through Observation

Next time you go to a store, a restaurant, or a gas station, pay attention to see if mistakes happen. Pay special attention to the way the employee handled the mistake and then discuss the information with the rest of the class.

1. Place_____

The mistake the employee made:_____

_____

What the employee did to fix the mistake:_____

_____

What the employee said:_____

_____

2. Place_____

The mistake the employee made:_____

_____

What the employee did to fix the mistake:_____

_____

What the employee said:_____

_____

3. Place_____

The mistake the employee made:_____

_____

What the employee did to fix the mistake:_____

_____

What the employee said:_____

_____

Chapter
4
Dealing With
Complaints

"Excuse me. There are onions on my hamburger."

OVERVIEW

Sometimes customers have complaints. When this happens, service employees need to know what to do: Should they give the customer his money back? Give him or her another item? Offer to take care of whatever is wrong?

Sometimes it is not possible to make the customer happy. The customer may be unreasonable and the store may have certain rules that the employee needs to follow. In any case experienced service employees stay friendly and calm when they have to handle complaints. Here are some examples of customer complaints:

1. How come there are onions on my hamburger? I thought I told you "no onions."

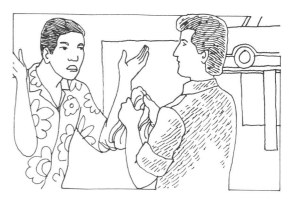

2. The new brakes you guys installed aren't working. I put my foot on the pedal and nothing happens.

3. I bought this hair spray here yesterday and it won't spray.

4. This food is cold. And the coffee tastes funny.

5. I have been waiting here for half an hour, and I still haven't gotten any service.

6. How do you expect me to sleep when there is a party going on next door?

INTERACTING

At a Fast Food Counter

Handling complaints can be difficult, especially if the customer is angry or unfriendly. You will hear two different interactions between a customer and a counter clerk in a fast food restaurant. Listen and decide which employee does a better job handling the complaint.

Interaction I: I didn't hear you say that.

What is Your Opinion?

Circle the answer that you think is best.

1. The counter clerk was polite enough. The customer was wrong; she never said "no onions."

2. The counter clerk was not very polite, but that's okay, because the customer was so mean.

3. The counter clerk was rude to the customer. He should continue to be polite even if the customer is wrong.

4. Other: _____

Discuss your answer with the other people in your group and explain your reasons.

_____

_____

Comprehension Questions

1. Where does the interaction take place?

2. Who is talking?

3. What is the problem?

4. What does the customer order?

5. What questions does the counter clerk ask when the customer orders?

6. The customer complains. What does the customer say?

7. What is the counter clerk's answer to the complaint?

8. Does the counter clerk agree with the customer? What does the clerk say?

9. Is the interaction between the customer and the counter clerk a friendly interaction? Explain.

10. In your opinion, what will the customer tell the manager?

Interaction II: Would you like another hamburger?

Comprehension Questions

1. Is the fast food clerk doing a good job? Why or why not?
2. Where is the interaction taking place?
3. What questions does the counter clerk ask?
4. What complaint does the customer have?
5. What does the counter clerk say when the customer complains?
6. What offer does the counter clerk make?
7. Does the customer like that offer? What does he say?
8. What does the counter clerk say next?
9. What does the counter clerk tell the manager?
10. What does the manager tell the counter person to do?
11. What does the counter clerk ask the customer?
12. What is the last thing the counter clerk says?

Let's Compare

What is the difference between the clerk in Interaction I and the clerk in Interaction II?

_____

_____

_____

Now It's Your Turn

Excuse me, but . . . .

Practice the customer/clerk interaction. One student is the waiter/waitress, another student is the customer. A third student is the manager.

ROLES

The customer: Orders food.
Does not like something about the food.
Complains to the waiter.

The waiter/waitress: Takes the order.
Finds out what customer wants.
Listens to the complaint.
Reports complaint to manager.
Listens to manager.
Does what manager tells him to do.

The manager: Listens to report from waiter.
Tells waiter what to do or talks to customer directly.

Role Play Checklist

Watch other students play the role of waiter/waitress and customer. How did the waiter/waitress handle the complaint? Did he/she do a good job or did he/she argue with the customer? Circle either *yes* or *no* and discuss your answers with the class.

1. The waiter/waitress tried to find out what the customer wanted. yes/no

2. The waiter/waitress repeated the order. yes/no

3. The waiter/waitress listened to the complaint. yes/no

4. The waiter/waitress sounded friendly when he/she answered the complaint. yes/no

5. The waiter/waitress argued with the customer. yes/no

6. The waiter/waitress tried to be helpful. yes/no

7. The waiter/waitress offered to talk to the manager. yes/no

8. The waiter/waitress clearly explained the problem to the manager. yes/no

9. The waiter/waitress carefully explained to the customer what the manager said. yes/no

10. The waiter/waitress sounded friendly and professional. yes/no

Match-Up

Experienced service employees apologize and give explanations when they hear a complaint.

IN A RESTAURANT OR STORE

Customer: This is ridiculous. I have been standing in this line for 20 minutes.

Employee: I'm sorry you had to wait so long. Three of our employees are sick today and it's a very busy day.

AT AN AUTOMOTIVE GARAGE

Customer: I brought my car here yesterday for a tune-up, but it is still not running right.

Repair person: I'm sorry. Why don't you leave the car here today and we'll have another look at it.

Match the customer complaints with the clerk responses.

_____ **1.** I have been here for fifteen minutes, and I have not gotten any service.

_____ **2.** You gave me an appointment for Thursday, but I have class on Thursday.

_____ **3.** You said you would be here to repair my TV at 2 o'clock. Now it's almost 3:30.

_____ **4.** You used to carry Clean Face Shaving Cream, and now I can't find it.

_____ **5.** My tire is low, and it needs air, but your air hose is not working.

_____ **6.** I don't think you gave me the correct change.

_____ **7.** There are only two towels in my room. That's not enough for me. I will need more towels than that.

_____ **8.** I bought these light bulbs here last week, but two of them don't work.

_____ **9.** This coffee tastes absolutely terrible.

_____ **10.** What do you mean the lot is full? I absolutely have to park here. I'm late for a meeting.

CLERK RESPONSES

a) I'm sorry, but that's the only opening we have this week.

b) I'm sorry. The last job took longer than I thought and traffic was heavy coming over here.

c) I'm sorry. Let me count it again.

d) I'm sorry. We discontinued it (we don't carry it any more). Not enough people were buying it.

e) I'm sorry. We have been really busy. I will tell your waitress right away.

f) I'm sorry, it's broken. We haven't had time to fix it yet.

g) I'm sorry, I can't exchange them without a sales receipt.

h) I'm sorry, we haven't had any other complaints. We are making a fresh pot right now, or would you rather have some tea?

i) I'm very sorry. But we are not allowed to take extra cars. You might be able to find a place down the street.

j) I'm sorry. I will call housekeeping right away. They will bring over some extra ones for you.

LEARNING THE LANGUAGE

Customer complaints are quite common. Experienced employees know how to handle complaints without getting angry or embarrassed.

There are different ways to respond to a complaint. For example in a restaurant you may hear the following:

Customer: There are onions on my hamburger. I can't eat onions; I have an important meeting this afternoon.

Waiter: Let me take the hamburger back to the kitchen. I'll be right back with a plain one.

Here are some other ways of handling complaints:

1. You can make an exchange.

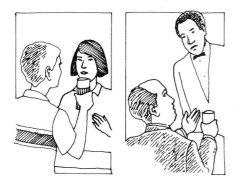

Customer: I bought this can of shaving cream here yesterday, but the foam doesn't come out right.

Store clerk: I'm sorry. Why don't you pick out another one?

Customer: This glass has lipstick marks on it.

Waiter: I'm terribly sorry. Let me get you a clean one right away.

2. You can offer to redo the job.

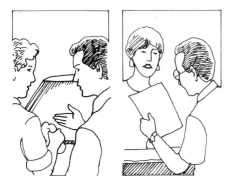

Customer: I don't think you did a very good job cleaning that window. It still has streaks on it.

Attendant: I'm sorry. Let me go over that one more time.

Customer: This copy came out kind of crooked.

Copy clerk: You're right. It is crooked. Let me redo it for you.

3. You can suggest another item, if possible.

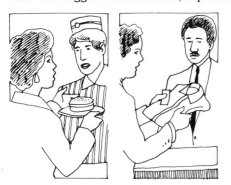

Customer: This fish sandwich smells funny.

Counter clerk: I'm terribly sorry. Would you like to order something else?

Customer: I bought this shirt here a few days ago as a present, but it's the wrong size. Here's my sales receipt.

Sales clerk: Why don't you go ahead and pick out a different size?

4. You can explain that there is nothing you can do.

Customer: Our room is really very noisy. We would like to have something a little quieter.

Desk clerk: I am *really* sorry. I know that the street is a little noisy, but *we* don't have anything *else* available. But things get much more quiet after 7 o'clock.

Customer: I couldn't possibly get my car into that space over there. Don't you have any bigger spaces?

Attendant: I'm sorry, but that is the only space that we have left.

5. You can explain store policy.

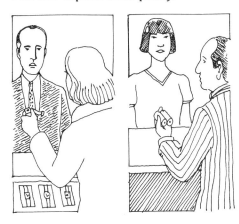

Customer: The beeper on this watch is driving me crazy. I would like to get my money back.

Clerk: I'm sorry, but we only allow exchanges, no refunds. Let me show you some watches with different beepers.

Customer: I bought these batteries here a couple of days ago, but they are the wrong kind.

Clerk: I'm sorry, but without a sales receipt I can't give you an exchange.

Quick Practice

Study the situation below. Then decide what the service person should do. Circle the best answer.

1. At a Restaurant

Customer: Excuse me, but this fork is dirty.

The waiter should say:

a) Would you like a clean fork?

b) Let me get you another one right away.

c) Let me redo it.

2. At a Donut Shop

Customer: I just bought this donut from you. It's stale.

The clerk should say:

a) I'm sorry, but you need a sales receipt. If you don't have one, I can't exchange it.

b) I'm sorry, but that's impossible. All of our donuts are fresh. We baked them this morning.

c) I'm sorry. Our donuts are usually fresh. Would you like your money back or would you like to pick out another kind?

3. At a Parking Lot

Customer: What do you mean, parking costs $1 an hour? Last week it was only 75 cents.

The parking lot attendant should say:

a) I'm sorry, but the price went up. There's nothing I can do. I'm sorry.

b) Let me talk to the manager to see what I can do.

c) I'm sorry. You can always park someplace else if you don't like it.

On Your Own

One person will be the customer, the other is the service employee. The customer makes a complaint and the service employee responds. Use the examples at the beginning of the chapter as your guide.

Customer: This coffee is cold.

Waiter: I'm sorry. I'll bring you a fresh cup right away.

---

1. Customer complains that a soda tastes funny.
Waiter: I'm sorry. Would you like...

2. Customer complains that a glass has a crack in it.
Waiter: I'm sorry. Let me...

3. Customer complains a shirt she bought is too large.
Sales clerk: I'm sorry. Why don't you...

4. Customer complains that a cigarette lighter is not working.
Store clerk: I'm sorry. Why don't you...

5. Customer complains that the TV in his room is not working.
Desk clerk: I'm sorry. Let me check with...

6. Customer complains that the bread is not fresh.
Store clerk: ...

7. Customer complains about onions on a hamburger.
Counter clerk: ...

8. Customer complains that a copy is smudged (dirty).
Copy clerk: ...

9. Customer complains that a window is dirty.
Gas station attendant: ...

10. Customer complains that his hamburger tastes strange.
Waiter: ...

MAKING IT WORK

Discussion/Vocabulary

Customers may complain about food, unfriendly or slow service, broken equipment, long waits, *etc.*

In a motel you may hear the following complaints:

- There are not enough towels.
- The sink is dripping.
- A light bulb went out.
- The carpet is dirty.
- The television does not work.
- A baby is crying next door.
- There are not enough hangers in the closet.

What kind of complaints would you hear in the following places? Make a guess and discuss your answers with others in the group. Then make a list. For each case, decide if the complaint is reasonable or unreasonable.

1. Requests in a Restaurant

Reasonable	*Unreasonable*
_____	_____
_____	_____
_____	_____
_____	_____

2. Requests in a Department Store

Reasonable   *Unreasonable*

_____   _____

_____   _____

_____   _____

_____   _____

3. Requests in a Copy Store

Reasonable   *Unreasonable*

_____   _____

_____   _____

_____   _____

_____   _____

4. Requests in a Parking Lot

Reasonable   *Unreasonable*

_____   _____

_____   _____

_____   _____

5. Requests at a Full-Service Gas Station

Reasonable   *Unreasonable*

_____   _____

_____   _____

_____   _____

_____   _____

Communication Skills Practice

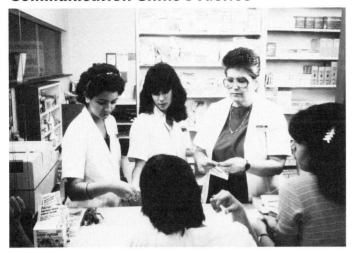

Choose a situation. One student is the customer and the other is the clerk, waiter, or salesperson.

ROLES

Customer: Makes a complaint

Employee: Says "I'm sorry"
Gives explanation, if possible
Explains what he/she will do next

The customer starts with: "Excuse me."

1. In a Restaurant

Customer: Calls over waiter.
Complains that his eggs are too soft.

Waiter: Apologizes.
Will take eggs back to the cook.
Will take only a few minutes.
Offers to bring some more coffee or tea in the meantime.

A few minutes later:
Brings eggs back ("Here you are.")
Explains that cook cooked them some more.
Asks if eggs look okay?
Says: "Enjoy your breakfast."

2. At a Gas Station

Customer: Bought eight dollars worth of gas.
Gave clerk a twenty dollar bill.
Complains that she only got change for a ten.

Clerk: Says: "Let me double-check."
Explains that customer was right.
Apologizes.
Says: "Here are your ten dollars."
Apologizes again.

3. In a Fast Food Restaurant

Customer: Explains that he just ordered a hamburger.

Complains that hamburger is cold.

Counter Apologizes.

Clerk: Offers to give guest another hamburger.

Apologizes again.

4. In a Convenience Store

Customer: Bought a bottle of hairspray yesterday.

Bottle won't spray right.
(The nozzle is clogged up.)

Clerk: Apologizes.

Tries to spray.

Says: "You're right. It's not working."
Suggests that customer pick out another spray.

Tries the new bottle.
Says: "Here you are. You're all set."

5. In a Motel

Customer: Explains what room he is in.
Explains that he has to get up early for an important meeting.

Complains that he can't sleep because people next door are having a loud party.

Asks the desk clerk to do something.

Desk clerk: Apologizes
Will talk to the people in the next room right away.

Says: "I'll take care of it. I'll make sure things quiet down so that you can sleep."

Wishes customer good night.

6. At a Parking Lot

Customer: Drives into the parking lot in the afternoon.

Explains that he already has a ticket.

Attendant: Apologizes.
The ticket is no good.
The policy (rule) is "no in and out on the same ticket."
Points to the sign.

Apologizes again.
Customer has to buy another ticket.

7. In a Grocery Store

Customer: Explains she just bought cigarettes and coffee.
It cost $5.19.

She gave the clerk ten dollars.
Complains that she got nine cents and four dollars in change.

Clerk: Says: "Let me double-check the price."

Explains that customer was right.
Apologizes.

Explains the right amount. Counts it out.

8. At a Customer's Home

Customer: Explains that she has been waiting all morning.
Explains that she expected the repair person at 11 o'clock.
Explains that it is now 2 o'clock in the afternoon.
Complains that the repair person is 3 hours late.

Repair Person: Apologizes
Explains that the morning job took longer than expected.
Explains that there was an accident on the way over.
Says: "I'm really sorry you had to wait so long."
Explains that he will get to work right away.

Moving Up Faster

Some complaints are easy to handle. Others are more difficult. Sometimes customers make unreasonable demands or get angry at the clerks. Experienced employees stay calm even when customers shout at them. They try to act in a professional manner no matter what the circumstances.

Role play the following situations. Handle the angry customer in the same way as a professional would.

ROLES

Customer: Makes a complaint.
Gets upset and angry.

Employee: Does not get upset.
Gives explanations.
Tries to keep the customer calm.

---

1. At a Donut Shop

Customer: Explains that he gave clerk twenty dollars.

Complains that he only got change for ten.

Insists that he paid with a "twenty."
Demands to talk to the manager.

Clerk: Says she will double-check.
Apologizes and explains to customer that he only gave her ten dollars.

Explains that manager is not in. Offers to take customer's name and phone number.

Explains that she will tell manager to double-check the cash register.

Explains that the manager will call the customer if there was a mistake.

2. At a Jewelry Store

Customer: Explains that he bought the watch the week before.

Explains that it was a present for his girlfriend, but that she broke up with him and now he has no use for the watch.

Explains that he would like to get his money back.

Explains why he does not want to keep the watch.

Explains why he doesn't want an exchange.

Clerk: Says: "I'm sorry about your girlfriend, but..."

Explains that the store does not give refunds.
Explains that store only allows exchanges.

Suggests that customer keep watch for next girlfriend.

Suggests that customer get a watch for a relative or someone's birthday.

Apologizes again and explains again that he cannot give the customer his money back.

Offers to let customer talk to the manager.

Progress Report

Handling complaints can be very tricky. Sometimes employees can do something about the complaint, but, at other times, it may not be possible to keep the customer happy. In either case, employees need to listen very carefully to the complaint and ask questions to make sure they understand all the details of the complaint. When there is nothing they can do about the complaint, employees should give a reason such as explaining store policy. Above all, employees should *never* argue with the customer. If employees are not sure how to handle a complaint, they should check with the manager. Important complaints always need to be reported.

How well did your group do in handling complaints? Fill out a progress report for the people you observed.

What did the service employee do? Check the appropriate box.

	DID WELL	SOME PROBLEMS	NEEDS MORE PRACTICE
1. Listened carefully; looked customer in the eye; asked questions to get important information.			
2. Explained reason where necessary; offered to ask manager.			
3. Clearly explained complaint to manager.			
4. Sounded professional and did not argue with the customer.			

Overall evaluation:

_____ Fantastic! This person is ready to go to work.

_____ Pretty good under the circumstances!

_____ Not bad. With a little practice, this person will do well.

Case Study

Discuss the following case and decide what Minh should do.

Minh is working for an automotive garage. One Saturday, the shop is very busy and the customers have to wait a long time. A customer comes up to Minh and says: "This is ridiculous. I was told my car would be ready at 1:00. It is now 2:30. I am a very busy person and I want my car fixed now."

What should Minh do?

1. Minh should ignore the customer and continue his work. This is not Minh's problem.

2. Minh should say: "I'm sorry; I'm working as fast as I can. The more time I spend talking to you, the longer it is going to take me to finish this job."

3. Minh should say: "We are really busy today. Could you please talk to the manager about your car?"

4. Minh should say: "Believe me, I don't like this any more than you do. So, would you please be patient?"

5. Other: _____

_____

Discussion

In your opinion, which answers are good? Which answers could cause problems later on? Put a check (✔) next to the number. Discuss your opinion with others in your group. Be prepared to explain your reasons.

	GOOD	PROBLEM
1		
2		
3		
4		

What might be the best choice if Minh wants to keep his job?

_____

_____

_____

What should Minh remember for the next time?

_____

_____

_____

_____

GETTING DOWN TO BASICS

Calculating Skills

Quite often, service employees hear complaints about money. Sometimes customers say that the service employee overcharged them and didn't give them the correct amount of change. To avoid complaints, it is very important that service employees know how to make change and be very careful when they handle money.

 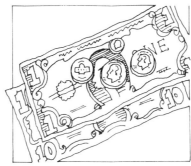

AT THE SELF-SERVICE GAS STATION
Customer gives attendant a twenty dollar bill. The gas costs $8.35.

The attendant counts back the change for the customer.
"That was $8.35. Here is your change.

Eight-fifty,	(hands customer a nickel and a dime)
nine,	(hands customer two quarters)
ten dollars,	(hands customer a dollar)
and ten makes twenty."	(hands customer a ten dollar bill)

Some establishments have cash registers that show how much change the customer gets.

The gas costs:	$7.35
The customer gives the attendant:	$10.00
The cash register says:	$2.65 (change)
The attendant says:	"Two sixty-five is your change."
"Here's two,	(hands the customer two dollar bills)
two-fifty,	(hands the customer two quarters)
two sixty-five."	(hands customer a dime and a nickel)

Practice I: The Attendant Counts Back Change

How does the clerk count back change for the following amounts when the customer gives him $20.00?

1. TOTAL COST: $4.62
2. TOTAL COST: $9.73
3. TOTAL COST: $2.17

4. TOTAL COST: $14.00
5. TOTAL COST: $18.01

Practice II: The Cash Register Calculates Change

What does the clerk do and say when he gives back the following change?

1. CHANGE: $2.54
2. CHANGE: $7.07

3. CHANGE: $6.92
4. CHANGE: $11.78

Reading

Many times when service employees handle complaints, they must explain store rules or company rules. Store and company rules are also called "policies." Sometimes, policies are listed on signs so that customers are aware of them.

Read the following signs as fast as you can and decide where you might find such a policy. More than one answer is possible. Work as fast as you can.

POLICY	PLACE
1. NO REFUND WITHOUT SALES RECEIPT	_____
2. EXCHANGES ONLY	_____
3. NO IN AND OUT ON SAME TICKET	_____
4. NOT RESPONSIBLE FOR ITEMS LEFT ON PREMISES	_____
5. NO BILLS LARGER THAN $20 ACCEPTED AT NIGHT	_____
6. NO SHOES, NO SHIRT, NO SERVICE	_____
7. CHECK OUT TIME 12 O'CLOCK NOON	_____
8. THERE IS A 50 CENT CHARGE ON ALL PHONE CALLS	_____
9. NO EXCHANGES UNLESS ACCOMPANIED BY A SALES RECEIPT	_____
10. 15% SERVICE CHARGE AND STATE SALES TAX WILL BE ADDED TO ORDER	_____
11. NO REFUNDS ON SELF-SERVICE COPIES	_____

Quick Practice

You are handling a complaint in a store, a motel, a parking lot, or a restaurant.
Reread the policies and decide which policy would apply in each case.

Clerk: I'm sorry that you made too many copies by mistake, but I can't charge you
less. Our policy states: *No refunds on self service copies.*

---

1. I'm sorry, but we cannot accept your $50 bill. Our store policy states: _____

   _____

2. I'm sorry, but you have to pay for parking again. Our policy is: _____

   _____

3. I'm sorry, I can't give you your money back. But the store policy is: _____

   _____

4. I'm sorry you are upset about the extra charge on your room service bill. But here it says on your

   menu: _____

   _____

5. I'm sorry, but we can't let you into the restaurant with bare feet. Our policy says: _____

   _____

6. I'm sorry, but you can't stay in your room this afternoon. The policy is: _____

   _____

7. I'm sorry, but we can't watch the coats in the coat room. I'll look for it but the sign says: _____

   _____

Reading/Writing

Sometimes the manager is not available when a customer has a complaint. In these cases, the employee may have to leave a note for the manager.

Study the complaint below and role play the situation. Then write a note to the manager and explain the situation.

You are a desk clerk at a small motel. On March fifteenth, Friday evening at nine-thirty, Frank Babayan, a hotel guest from room 317 comes to the desk to make a complaint. The guest tells you that he just came back from dinner and went to his room. When he got there, he noticed that his watch was missing from the room. He had left the watch on the night table. The guest thinks that a hotel employee stole the watch. The guest demands to talk to the manager.

The manager is not at the motel and cannot be reached by phone. Tell the customer that you will write down the complaint and give it to the manager. Promise that the manager will call the guest in the morning.

Fill out the complaint form below. Write down the most important information. Explain to the "guest" what you are doing. Double-check with the guest to make sure you have the right information.

Date: _____

To: _____

From: _____

Re: *Customer Complaint*

Time of complaint: _____

Nature of complaint: _____

_____

_____

Name of customer: _____ Room: _____

Customer was told: _____

_____

_____

_____

_____
        (Signature)

OUT IN THE REAL WORLD

Assignment I: Learning from Experience

Have you ever had a complaint in a store, a restaurant, hotel, gas station, or parking lot? Have your friends or relatives ever had a complaint? Tell what happened and describe the complaint in detail. Explain how the salesperson reacted.

Assignment II: Learning through Observation

Next time you go to a store, a restaurant, or a coffee shop, pay special attention to see if you hear any complaints. Write down the information and then discuss it with the other students in the class.

1. Place _____

What the customer said: _____

_____

The employee's reaction: _____

_____

Did the customer seem satisfied? Why or why not? Explain.

_____

_____

2. Place _____

What the customer said: _____

_____

The employee's reaction: _____

_____

Did the customer seem satisfied? Why or why not? Explain.

_____

_____

3. Place _____

What the customer said: _____

_____

The employee's reaction: _____

_____

Did the customer seem satisfied? Why or why not? Explain.

_____

_____

Chapter 5

Dealing With Special Requests

"Let me talk to the manager to see what we can do."

OVERVIEW

Sometimes customers make *special requests*. When this happens the *employee* has to decide whether to say *yes* and grant the request or whether to say *no* and turn the request down. Here are some examples of special requests:

1. Could I stay an hour past check-out time, please?

2. Could I have the mashed potatoes instead of the rice with the special?

3. Could you write the receipt for two dollars more?

4. I don't have any cash. Could I write you a check?

5. Could I use your phone? This is an emergency.

6. Could I have a special discount?

INTERACTING

In the Motel Lobby

Dealing with special requests is not always easy. You will hear two different interactions between a hotel guest and a desk clerk. Listen carefully and decide how well each handles the special request.

Interaction I: I'm sorry. No exceptions.

What is Your Opinion?

Circle the answer that you think is best.

1. The desk clerk was very impolite. He should let the guest stay until his wife comes back.
2. The desk clerk did a good job. It is against the rules to let guests stay past check-out time.
3. The guest should not ask special favors. This puts the desk clerk in a bad position. The guest was wrong. The desk clerk was right.

4. Other:_____

_____

Discuss your answer with the other people in your group and explain your reasons.

Comprehension Questions

1. Where does the interaction take place?
2. Who is talking?
3. What problem does the guest have?
4. What does the guest want?
5. What reasons does the guest give?
6. What does the desk clerk say?
7. What reasons does the guest clerk give?
8. How does the guest feel at the end of the conversation? Why?

Interaction II: Let me talk to the manager to see what we can do.

Comprehension Questions

1. Did the desk clerk handle the special request well? Explain.
2. What is the guest's problem? What does he want?
3. What is the desk clerk's first response?
4. What does the guest tell the manager?
5. What is the manager's response?
6. What reason does the manager give for his decision?
7. What does the desk clerk tell the guest?
8. The guest makes another request. What is it?
9. How does the desk clerk respond?
10. Does the desk clerk try to keep the guest happy? Explain.

Let's Compare

The two desk clerks handled the situation in a different way. What did each do or not do? Look at the list below and check what each desk clerk did.

		CLERK I	CLERK II
a)	Explained policy		
b)	Offered to ask the manager		
c)	Explained the problem to the manager		
d)	Let the manager know that he/she understood		
e)	Apologized to the guest		
f)	Explained to guest why he couldn't stay longer		
g)	Made another suggestion (explained what the guest could do instead)		
h)	Offered to help guest		
i)	Made guest feel welcome		

Now It's Your Turn

Let Me Talk to the Manager to See What We Can Do.

Practice the customer interaction between the guest, the desk clerk, and the manager. The desk clerk tries to be friendly, but firm.

ROLES

Guest: Wants to stay in the room past check-out time. Gives reason.

Desk Clerk: Listens to guest.
Explains policy.
Offers to talk to manager.
Explains manager's decision.

Manager: Listens to desk clerk.
Makes a decision.
Tells the desk clerk what to say to the guest.

Role Play Checklist

Watch other students play the role of the guest, the desk clerk, and the manager. Did the clerk stay friendly but firm? Circle *yes* or *no* and discuss your answers with the class.

1. The desk clerk listened politely while customer explained problem.   yes/no
   Did he/she maintain eye contact?   yes/no

2. The desk clerk explained motel policy.   yes/no
   Did he/she sound friendly but firm?   yes/no
   Did he/she sound clear?   yes/no

3. The desk clerk talked to the manager.   yes/no
   Did he/she explain the problem clearly?   yes/no

4. Did the desk clerk explain the manager's decision?   yes/no

5. Was the guest satisfied with the decision?   yes/no

Match-Up

Many times an employee can keep a customer happy by saying yes to a request. But at other times, an employee may have to say "no." In these cases, experienced employees usually apologize ("I'm sorry.") and explain why the request cannot be granted.

AT A SELF-SERVICE GAS STATION

Customer: Excuse me, but my car keeps dying. Could you check that out for me?

Attendant: I'm sorry. We don't have any mechanics at this station. But there is a garage just down the street. Maybe they can help you.

Match the special request with the appropriate reasons for saying no.

CUSTOMER'S QUESTIONS

_____ **1.** Could I get decaffeinated coffee?

_____ **2.** Could I get this fish broiled instead of fried?

_____ **3.** Could you leave the parking spots next to my car empty? It's new and I don't want anyone banging into it.

_____ **4.** While you are here fixing the sink, could you have a look at the TV? It's making funny noises.

_____ **5.** Could you please not cash that check right away? I want to deposit my paycheck first.

_____ **6.** Could you change that five dollar bill for me, please? I need to go to the laundromat.

CLERK'S ANSWERS

a) I'm sorry, but we only serve regular.

b) I'm sorry, but if the lot fills up, we will need to use every single space.

c) I'm sorry. But we can only open the register if we ring up a purchase.

d) I'm sorry, but for bookkeeping purposes we have to take all checks that come in to the bank at the end of the day.

e) I'm sorry, ma'am, but I know nothing about electronics, so I can't really help you.

f) I'm sorry, but in order to save time, our cook has to prepare all the fish the same way.

LEARNING THE LANGUAGE

There are different ways of responding to a request.

Part I: Saying *Yes* or *No* to a Request.

Here are some common ways of handling a request:

1. You can grant the request right away.

Customer: Could I please have some extra ketchup with my french fries?

Counter clerk: Certainly. How many packets would you like?

Customer: Could you write me a receipt for the parking fee?

Parking Attendant: Sure. Just a second.

2. You can explain what will happen if you grant the request.

Customer: I need to wear that suit for a party tonight. Do you think you could have it cleaned by this afternoon?

Dry Cleaner: Yes, we can, but it will cost slightly more.

Customer: Could I have a freshly made hamburger instead of one of the ones sitting on the counter?

Fast Food Counter Clerk: Certainly, if you can wait a couple of minutes.

Sometimes it is not possible to grant the request and the employee has to say *no*. In such a situation, you can do the following:

3. You can say you're sorry and explain why you can't grant the request.

Customer: Could I please have cottage cheese instead of french fries with my hamburger?

Waiter: I'm really sorry. We can't make substitutions. But you can order a side order of cottage cheese if you like.

Hotel Guest: Could you come in and chat with me for a while? I miss my family and need someone to talk to.

Maid: I'm sorry, sir. But we are not allowed to be in the room with guests.

Quick Practice

Respond to the special requests below. In each case, decide if you want to grant the request or say *no*. Remember to apologize and give a reason if you decide to say *no*. Check examples for ideas.

1. Customer: Could you help me pack my things, please? My airplane leaves in an hour and a half and I am late for the airport.

Maid:_____

_____

2. Customer: Could you leave the onions and the peppers out of my omelette and put in tomatoes instead?

Waiter:_____

_____

3. Customer: Could I have fresh french fries please, instead of the ones you have sitting over there?

Counter Clerk:_____

_____

4. Motel Guest: Could we stay past check-out time? Our children are having so much fun in the pool and they don't want to go home.

Desk Clerk:_____

_____

5. Customer: Could I get some extra sugar with my coffee?

Counter Clerk:_____

_____

6. Customer: Could you please not park any cars next to my car? It's brand new, and I'm afraid that it will get scratched.

Parking Lot Attendant:_____

_____

7. Customer: After you have finished checking my refrigerator, could you look at the sink? The faucet keeps leaking and I don't know what's wrong.

Repair Person:_____

_____

Part II: Reporting Requests to the Supervisor

Sometimes, the employee may not be sure whether to grant a request or not. In such a case, it may be best to:

a) politely explain to the customer what the rules are

b) offer to double-check with the manager

c) briefly explain the problem to the manager

d) explain to the customer what the manager said

e) apologize and give a reason if the answer was negative

f) suggest an alternative to the customer

Study the example below.

IN A RESTAURANT

Customer: Oh my goodness, I just realized that I left my wallet at home. But I do have my checkbook with me. Could I just pay for the food with a check?

Waiter: Well, normally, we accept cash only, no checks, but let me double-check with the manager to see what we can do. I'll be right back.

Waiter to Manager: I have a customer who says he forgot his wallet, so he can't pay cash. He does have his checkbook though. Can we accept his check?

Manager: Ask him to leave his checkbook as security and tell him to go home and get the cash.

Waiter to Customer: Sir, the manager said he would be happy to let you go home and get your wallet, if you could leave your checkbook here as security.

Quick Practice

Study the following customer requests and report them to the supervisor. Use the examples for ideas.

Guest: Could I leave my bags here while I go shopping?

Clerk to Manager: The guest wants to know if he can leave his bags while he goes shopping.

Customer: Could you write up the receipt for two dollars more? I forgot to get a receipt last time.

Cashier to Manager: The customer wants to know if we can write up the receipt for two dollars over. He says he forgot to get one last time.

---

1. *Customer:* Could I get fruit instead of french fries with the hamburger plate? I'm on a diet.

Waiter to Manager: _____

_____

2. *Customer:* Could your bag girl please come with me to my house and help me carry the groceries upstairs? I'll give her a ride back.

Checker to Manager: _____

_____

3. *Customer:* My driver's license got stolen. Could you please accept this check anyway? I have some other kinds of ID.

Cashier to Manager: _____

_____

4. *Guest:* Could you please move me to another room? The baby next door has been crying for hours and I can't get to sleep.

Desk Clerk to Manager: _____

_____

5. *Customer:* I know that you are already closed but I ran out of gas 1/2 mile down the street. Could you just let me have a gallon of gas so I can make it home?

Attendant to Station Manager: _____

_____

6. *Customer:* Could I have the dinner salad with my dinner, instead of the soup?

Waiter to Manager: _____

_____

7. *Customer:* Could I please use your phone for a minute? It's kind of an emergency.

Store Clerk to Manager: _____

_____

8. *Customer:* Could you give me a discount on these copies? They really did not come out very clean.

Copy Clerk to Manager: _____

_____

9. *Customer:* I know you usually don't allow exchanges without a receipt, but this tie I bought has a hole and I don't have another one to wear to my meeting. Could you please exchange it?

Salesperson to Department Manager: _____

_____

10. *Customer:* Could I just park here for a minute for free? I just need to run into this office. I'll be right back.

Parking Lot Attendant to Manager: _____

_____

MAKING IT WORK

Discussion/Vocabulary

There are many different kinds of special requests that a customer or a guest might make. Some of these requests might be reasonable (a hotel guest requests extra towels), others may be unreasonable (a customer at an automotive garage wants a ride home from the repair person). What special requests might a customer or a hotel guest make?

Make a guess and discuss your answers with others in your group. Then make a list. For each case decide if the request is reasonable or unreasonable.

1. Requests in a Restaurant

        Reasonable   *Unreasonable*

_____   _____

_____   _____

_____   _____

2. Requests in a Department Store

        Reasonable   *Unreasonable*

_____   _____

_____   _____

_____   _____

3. Requests in a Copy Store

        Reasonable   *Unreasonable*

_____   _____

_____   _____

_____   _____

4. Requests in a Parking Lot

        Reasonable   *Unreasonable*

_____   _____

_____   _____

_____   _____

5. Requests at a Full-Service Gas Station

        Reasonable   *Unreasonable*

_____   _____

_____   _____

_____   _____

Communication Skills Practice

Choose a situation. One student is the customer and the other is the clerk, waiter, or salesperson.

ROLES

Customer: Makes a special request

Employee: Says "I'm sorry"
Explains policy
Offers to double-check with the manager
Conveys manager's decision to customer
Suggests alternative

The employee starts with: "May I help you?"

1. In a Motel

Guest:	Wants to stay in room past check-out time. Explains that she is waiting for an important business call.
Desk Clerk:	Apologizes, explains check-out time, and offers to double-check with manager.
Manager:	Explains that room needs to be cleaned for next guest. Suggests that guest wait in lobby or bar, instead.
Desk Clerk:	Reports back to guest. Offers to find guest in bar or lobby when call comes in.

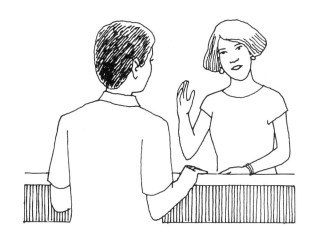

2. In a Restaurant

Customer:	Wants to put bill on credit card. Explains that he/she didn't know that restaurant does not accept credit cards.
Waiter:	Explains that restaurant normally does not accept credit cards; offers to talk to manager.
Manager:	Is unhappy. Tells waiter to ask customer to write a check. Tells waiter to be sure to write down driver's license number and credit card number.
Waiter:	Explains situation to customer.

3. In a Department Store

Customer: Wants to get money back on merchandise because merchandise is defective (explain). Explains that receipt was in purse, but purse was stolen.

*Store
Clerk:* Explains policy; offers to ask manager.

Manager: Explains that there are no exceptions to the policy.
Tells clerk to tell customer to pick out another item and make an exchange.

4. In a Parking Lot

Customer: Explains that he needs to give a friend an urgent message. He has no money for parking. Only wants to park for two minutes and will be right back.

Attendant: Explains that usually he is not allowed to let people park for free. Offers to talk to manager.

Manager: Suggests that the customer use a pay phone at a gas station to call his friend.

5. At a Gas Station

Customer: Explains that he just filled the tank; explains that he forgot credit card and has no cash.

Attendant: Explains that he is not sure what to do. Says he will check with manager.

Manager: Is unhappy. Tells attendant to keep customer's driver's license as security and tell customer to bring back cash later. Reminds attendant to ask for credit cards or cash first.

Attendant: Explains situation to customer.

6. At a Copy Store

Customer: Explains that she asked for receipt last time, but the clerk never gave her one. Wants receipt written for double the amount this time.

Clerk: Explains that she is not sure what to do; explains that she will talk to manager.

Manager: Explains that they can only write receipts for amount of purchase. Explains that all clerks are told to put receipts in bag with photo copies. Maybe the receipt was lost.

Clerk: Apologizes and explains situation to customer. Suggests that customer check bag each time she orders copies.

7. In a Motel

Customer: Wants discount on room; explains that TV was not working and that room was noisy.

Desk Clerk: Apologizes for TV not working; offers to talk to manager.

Manager: Explains that guest did not complain the night before; explains the guest could have had different room if he had complained sooner. Says "No discount."

Desk Clerk: Explains situation to customer.

8. At the Copy Store

Customer: Wants discount on copies because some of the copies are smudged.

Clerk: Explains that normally there is no discount; offers to check with manager;

Manager: Tells clerk to offer to redo the copies on a different machine.

Clerk: Repeats offer to customer.

Progress Report

Handling special requests requires special skills, especially if the request cannot easily be granted. Whenever they hear a request, employees need to listen carefully so that they will be able to respond correctly. When they have to say *no* to a request, employees need to remain friendly and sound cooperative. When turning down a request the employee should apologize and, if possible, explain why a special request cannot be granted. If the employee is not certain how to handle the request, he/she should ask the supervisor or manager. How well did the people in your group handle special requests? Fill out a progress report for the people you observed.

What did the service employee do? Check the appropriate box.

	DID WELL	SOME PROBLEMS	NEEDS MORE PRACTICE
1. Listened carefully; looked customer in the eye; sounded firm but friendly when saying "no."			
2. Explained reason where necessary; offered to ask manager.			
3. Clearly explained special request to manager.			
4. Apologized to guest and offered an alternative.			

Overall evaluation:

_____ Fantastic! This person is ready to go to work.

_____ Pretty good under the circumstances!

_____ Not bad. With a little practice this person will do well.

Case Study

Discuss the following case and decide what Carlos should do.

Carlos is working in an all-night gas station. One evening at around midnight, a young woman drives in and explains that she is about to run out of gas. She has no money. She would like to borrow two dollars worth of gas so that she can get home.

What should Carlos do?

1. Carlos should give the woman the gas, but ask her to leave a spare tire or something else until she comes back.
2. Carlos will be in trouble if he gives the woman the gas for free. He should tell her: "I'm very sorry, but I can't give you gas without money."
3. Carlos should give her twenty cents so she can call someone to pick her up.
4. Carlos should use his own money to give her the gas. He should also tell her that she is crazy to drive around by herself in the middle of the night.
5. Carlos should call the manager at home to find out what he should do.

6. Other:_____

_____

Discussion

In your opinion, which answers are good? Which answers could cause problems later on? Put a check (✓) next to the number. Discuss your opinion with others in your group. Be prepared to explain your reasons.

	GOOD	PROBLEM
1.		
2.		
3.		
4.		
5.		

Overall, what would be the best choice for Carlos? Why?

_____

_____

_____

What should Carlos remember for next time?

_____

_____

_____

GETTING DOWN TO BASICS

Calculating Skills

Sometimes guests and customers ask for special discounts on their bills. Discounts such as 10%, 20%, 50%, or 5% are not difficult to calculate even if you don't have a calculator to help you.

If an order is $10.00,
then a 10% discount would be $1.00.

If an order is $5.00,
then a 10% discount would be $.50 or fifty cents.

On $11.00,
a 10% discount would be $1.10.

How much would a 10% discount be on the following:

$20.00 ? _____

$4.00 ? _____

$100.00 ? _____

$400.00 ? _____

$430.00 ? _____

$431.50 ? _____

$35.70 ? _____

$2.70 ? _____

A 20% discount is of course twice as much as a 10% discount.

If an order is $10.00,
then a 10% discount would be $1.00,
and a 20% discount would be $2.00.

If an order is $5.00,
then a 10% discount would be .50 or fifty cents,
and a 20% discount would be $1.00.

How much would a 20% discount be on the following?

$200.00 ? _____

$50.00 ? _____

$75.00 ? _____

$4.00 ? _____

$150.00 ? _____

$10.50 ? _____

$11.40 ? _____

$113.00 ? _____

A 5% discount is half of a 10% discount.

_____

If an order is $10.00,
then a 10% discount would be $1.00,
and a 5% discount would be $.50 or fifty cents.

If an order is $5.00,
then a 10% discount would be $.50 or fifty cents,
and a 5% discount would be $.25 or twenty-five cents.

_____

How much would a 5% discount be on the following?

$10.00 ? _____

$100.00 ? _____

$50.00 ? _____

$5.00 ? _____

$140.00 ? _____

$65.40 ? _____

$6.10 ? _____

$.80 ? _____

A 50% discount means half off.

If an order is $10.00,
then a 50% discount would be half of $10.00 or $5.00.

If an order is $5.00,
then a 50% discount would be $2.50.

What would a 50% discount be on the following?

$100.00 ? _____

$500.00 ? _____

$40.40 ? _____

$34.00 ? _____

$140.80 ? _____

$80.20 ? _____

$4.10 ? _____

$.90 ? _____

SALE!
25% off
EVERYTHING

Writing

Many times, special requests come over the telephone and need to be written down. Listen to the special requests of the hotel guests and write the messages on the message pads below.

Date_____ Hour_____

To:_____

MESSAGES

From:_____

Phone: (_____) _____
        area code

Message:_____

_____

_____

_____

_____

Signed:_____

Date_____ Hour_____

To:_____

MESSAGES

From:_____

Phone: (_____) _____
        area code

Message:_____

_____

_____

_____

_____

Signed:_____

```
Date_____  Hour_____

To:_____

                    MESSAGES

From:_____

Phone:  (____)  _____
        area code

Message:_____
     .
_____

_____

_____

_____

            Signed:_____
```

OUT IN THE REAL WORLD

Assignment I: Learning from Experience

Have you or your friends ever made a special request in a store, a restaurant or a gas station? Explain the situation in detail. Talk about what you wanted and explain why. Then explain what the employee said.

Assignment II: Learning through Observation

When you go shopping, buy gas, or eat out, what kind of special requests do you make? What kind of special requests do other customers make? Are those requests granted or turned down? What reasons do employees give for turning down a request?

1. Special requests heard in fast food places or restaurants:

a) _____

b) _____

c) _____

d) _____

Which requests were turned down? What was the reason?

_____

_____

_____

_____

2. Special requests heard in stores:

a) _____

b) _____

c) _____

d) _____

Which requests were turned down? What was the reason?

_____

_____

_____

_____

3. Special requests heard in parking lots or gas stations:

a) _____

b) _____

c) _____

d) _____

Which requests were turned down? What was the reason?

_____

_____

_____

_____

Chapter 6

Moving Up the Career Ladder

"Could I talk to you about a raise?"

OVERVIEW

Most people who have jobs in public contact positions enjoy their work. Yet many of these employees plan to learn as much as they can about their jobs and then move up the career ladder. Others plan to get additional training and then switch to other jobs within the service industry. Still others use their jobs as a way to make money while they go to school to prepare for a different career. This is what some employees are doing:

1. Vanary is learning as much as he can about fast food. He hopes that the manager will ask him to be production manager soon.

2. Reynaldo works as a parking lot attendant while he takes accounting classes at a junior college.

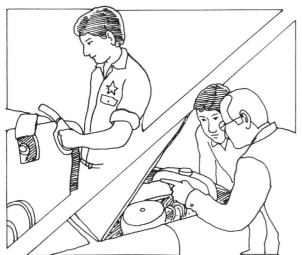

3. Tien pumps gas in a service station and garage while he studies to be an auto mechanic.

4. Cindy works as a maid in a motel while she goes to night school to improve her English.

5. Luz is production manager at a fast food restaurant. She plans to ask her boss to send her to management training so she can become an assistant manager.

6. Mai-Cee helps her uncle in his donut shop. She learns as much as she can about the job and saves all her money. She and her husband hope to buy their own shop one day.

7. Daniel works as a bus boy in a restaurant. He practices English every chance he gets. He plans to go to cooking school so he can work in the restaurant kitchen.

8. Sylvia is a waitress in a coffee shop. She plans to stay until she has enough experience to work in one of the larger restaurants where the tips are bigger.

Discussion

All the employees you have read about work in positions where they meet the public. Describe their jobs and discuss their plans for the future.

1. Mai-Cee works in a donut shop. Does she own the shop? What are her hopes for the future? How is she preparing for the future?

2. Where does Vanary work? What job is he hoping for next? How is he preparing for that job?

3. Cindy works as a maid. Do you think she has any plans for the future? Why is she going to night school?

4. Luz plans to become an assistant manager. What is her present job? How does she plan to become assistant manager?

5. Right now, Reynaldo works as a parking lot attendant. Do you think he will keep this job for the rest of his life? Explain.

6. Sylvia is a waitress. What are her plans for the future?

7. What is Daniel's ambition? How is he preparing for the future?

8. Will Tien keep the same job after he finishes his training? Explain.

9. What are your plans for the future?

10. What plans do the other people in your group have?

INTERACTING

Outside the Manager's Office

Many times the managers meet with their employees to talk about job performance and possible raises and promotions.

You will hear two different interactions between a manager and an employee. Listen and express your opinion of the two interactions.

Interaction I: I wonder what I did wrong.

What Is Your Opinion?

Circle the answer that you think is best.

1. Saroeun did the right thing. It is better to quit your job than to get fired.

2. Saroeun should have stayed to find out what the boss wanted. If she made a mistake, it is not the end of the world.

3. Saroeun was really stupid — maybe her boss wanted to praise her for the good work she was doing.

4. This is not a nice place for Saroeun. Going home was the right thing to do.

5. Other: _____

_____

Discuss the answer with the other people in your group and explain your reasons.

_____

_____

_____

_____

Comprehension Questions

1. Who is talking?
2. Where does the interaction take place?
3. What is going on?
4. In your opinion, why does the boss want to talk to Saroeun in his office? Circle the answer that matches your opinion.

   a) He wants to talk to her about a raise.

   b) He wants to see her because she did something wrong.

   c) He wants to talk to her about her work.

5. In Saroeun's opinion, why does the boss want to talk to her? What is she thinking?

6. What was the problem with Saroeun's lunch?
7. How will Saroeun feel if the boss talks to her about the lunch problem?
8. What does she plan to do?
9. What will she tell her family?
10. What does Saroeun's co-worker tell the boss?
11. What does the manager say about Saroeun?
12. What is his opinion of Saroeun?
13. In your opinion, did Sarouen do the right thing? Explain.

Interaction II: It's about time I got more money.

Comprehension Questions

1. Who is talking?
2. Where does the interaction take place?
3. What does Frank want?
4. What are his reasons?
5. Does the boss agree with Frank's reasons?
6. Where does the boss want to have the discussion? Why?

7. Why can't Frank meet his boss at four o'clock?
8. The boss talks about Frank's attitude. What does he say? Why?
9. Do you think the employee did the right thing? Explain.
10. What is your opinion of the boss?

Let's Compare

What is the difference between Frank and Saroeun?

_____

_____

_____

_____

_____

Match-Up

When looking for a promotion in your present job or looking for a new job, communication is important. Supervisors often discuss an employee's work with the employee. Receptionists often give information to would-be employees or applicants.

Supervisor: Overall, I'm happy with your work, but you need to show a little more initiative.

Employee: I'm not quite sure what you mean by initiative. What should I do differently?

Receptionist: We have some on-the-job training opportunities here for which you may qualify.

Applicant: What kind of jobs are available and how much do they pay?

Match the comments of the supervisors or receptionists with the appropriate response from the employee or applicant.

STATEMENTS BY A SUPERVISOR OR A RECEPTIONIST

_____ **1.** I would like to move you up, but your English is just not good enough yet.

_____ **2.** I'm thinking of letting you help a little at the front desk next week.

_____ **3.** We offer several math courses here at our school that might interest you. And there is no fee for the courses.

_____ **4.** Our institution offers several training courses for cooks at a very reasonable tuition rate.

_____ **5.** I'm sorry, I would like to move you up, but you are just not open and aggressive enough to make it as supervisor.

_____ **6.** You are doing a wonderful job. I am really impressed with how much you have learned since you started here.

_____ **7.** Thanks for filling out the application.

EMPLOYEE OR APPLICANT RESPONSES

a) Exactly how much do I have to pay? Do you have scholarships available? Do I get my money back if I find that the class isn't right for me?

b) Well, most of the time I don't have much trouble understanding what people are saying. Where do you think I need to improve?

c) I'm sorry you feel that way. What exactly would you like for me to do differently?

d) Thanks, I really appreciate that. I think you know that I am really responsible.

e) Thanks, that's good to hear. When would you consider me for a raise?

f) How often do these classes meet and how do I sign up? What happens if I don't like the class?

g) When will you make a decision about the position?

LEARNING THE LANGUAGE

Part I: Getting Information about Job Openings and Training Opportunities

Employees who have decided to get a better job often spend a great deal of time getting information about the kinds of jobs or training opportunities available in their area. Often they start out with a want ad in a paper or a notice in a school catalogue. Sometimes employees get information in person and sometimes they get information over the telephone. Here are some ways of getting information.

1. At the front desk in a school or a training institution

Man: Hi, my name is Frank Chang. I would like some information on your _____ classes.
                                 (English/business/accounting)

Receptionist: There's a catalogue over there. It explains all the classes we offer.

Man: Do you have a counselor that I could talk to? I have some questions that I would like to ask.

2. At the reception area of a company

Receptionist: May I help you?

Job Seeker: I saw your ad in the *Los Angeles Tribune* for cooks and waiters. Could I have an application to fill out?

OR

I am interested in the cook's job that you advertised. Could I make an appointment for an interview?

Quick Practice

One student will be the employee, another is the receptionist or the supervisor. Use the examples above as a guide.

1. You want to improve your chances for a better job and have decided to take classes at

_____.
   (name of school)

Talk to the receptionist and . . .

a) ask for a catalogue: _____

_____

b) ask when you can see a counselor: _____

_____

c) ask how much classes are: _____

_____

d) ask what you need to do to sign up for classes: _____

_____

2. You have seen a want ad in _____ for a job as _____
                                          (paper)   (job title)
with _____.
        (company)

a) explain where you saw the ad: _____

_____

b) explain what job you are interested in: _____

_____

c) ask if the job is still available: _____

_____

d) ask for an application: _____

_____

e) ask for an appointment for an interview: _____

_____

Part II: Talking to the Supervisor about a Raise or Promotion.

Sometimes, employees want to be promoted at the job where they are working. In these cases, the employees may talk to the supervisor to find out what their chances for advancement are.

At a job site:

Employee: I wonder if I could talk to you about my job when you have a few minutes?

Supervisor: Why don't you stop by my office after lunch?

When the employee meets the supervisor, he or she may say:

I really like my work, and I'm very interested in what I'm doing. Do you think I am doing a good job?

If the supervisor likes the employee's job performance, the employee may continue:

I'm glad you like my work. Will I be eligible for a raise soon?

OR

Could you tell me what I need to do to move up in the company? I really like it here, and would like to stay here.

If the supervisor thinks that the employee is *not* doing the best job possible, the employee may repeat what the supervisor said and ask for more details:

You said that I don't show enough *initiative*. I'm not sure what you mean.

OR

You said I don't care enough about my work. What could I do better?

Quick Practice

The teacher will be the supervisor. Students will be the employees. Use the examples on page 137 as your guide.

You decide that you have been working long and hard at the same job and you deserve a raise.

1. Ask if you could talk to the supervisor for a few minutes:

_____

2. Ask if she thinks you are doing a good job:

_____

If she says yes,

3. Ask when you could expect a raise: _____

_____

_____

4. Ask how you could move up in the company:

_____

_____

If she says no,

5. Ask her what the problem is: _____

_____

_____

6. Ask what you should do differently: _____

_____

_____

GETTING DOWN TO BASICS

Writing

When employees apply for a better job in a different company, they usually have to fill out an employment application. The same is often true for employees who want to move up in the same company. For this reason, many employees keep a record of their education and their skills and qualifications so that they will be ready when an employment opportunity comes up.

Fill out the employment application on the next page.

EMPLOYMENT APPLICATION

Date _____

Name: _____
      (last)   (first)   (middle)

Address: _____
      (No.)   (Street)   City   State   Zip Code

Home telephone _____ Social Security No. _____

Male _____ Female _____

Country of Citizenship? _____

Length of time in the U.S.? _____

EDUCATION

School	Grades completed	Diplomas/ Certificates
Grade School		
High School		
College		
Business or Vocational		
Other Training		

EMPLOYMENT HISTORY

List previous employment.

Position	From Mo/Yr	To Mo/Yr	Reason for Leaving

Skills Acquired through Work Experience or Volunteer Work

Skills	Place Acquired

Reading

Employees looking for better jobs often read want ads and job postings to get a good sense of available opportunities.

Read the job postings below and answer the questions that follow.

1. Production Leader at Fast Food Restaurant

Job description:	Coordinate work of fast food workers in kitchen and at counter. Help cook, assemble food, and serve food as necessary.
Salary:	$5.00; no benefits
Previous work experience:	Experience in fast food restaurant (cooking, assembling food, taking orders, cashiering)
Position available:	Varying shifts, 30 hrs. per week
Advancement possibilities:	Assistant manager with further on-the-job and company training; outside schooling to perfect English and math skills desirable.

2. Food Service Worker at Fast Food Restaurant

Job description:	Assemble and cook food; take customer orders, work register and clean kitchen and dining area as necessary.
Salary:	Minimum wage; no benefits
Previous work experience:	Desirable, but not necessary
Position available:	20 hrs, 3 p.m. to midnight, downtown mall
Advancement possibilities:	Move up to production manager with on-the-job training; assistant manager with further training and/or outside schooling.

3. Mechanic

Job description:	Performs repair work and preventive maintenance.
Salary:	Varies according to experience.
Previous work experience:	3 years experience, automotive training
Position available:	All shifts: department store automotive center
Advancement possibilities:	Service writer, shop supervisor

4. Front Desk Clerk at a Motel or Hotel

Job description: Clerk handles billing, reservations and scheduling procedures, and provides information as needed.

Previous work experience: Previous motel work, background in math and simple accounting procedures, good communication skills.

Position available: 3 p.m. to midnight, motel near airport

Salary: $15,000 to $18,000 a year

Advancement possibilities: Assistant manager/manager with further training

Comprehension Questions

1. What kind of work experience is required for the position of production leader in a fast food restaurant?

2. How much money will the mechanic make?

3. What kind of advancement possibilities will the food service worker have?

4. What duties will the front desk clerk need to perform?

5. What will be the work schedule for the production leader?

6. What position is open at the downtown mall?

7. Which job offers up to $18,000 a year in salary?

8. Which ad mentions "math skills desirable?"

9. For which position is previous work experience not necessary?

10. Which job requires "good communication skills?"

MAKING IT WORK

Discussion

Many times when people try to find a better job or try to start a new training program, they have to go through an interview. Usually the interviewer asks a number of questions that the applicant needs to answer.

What kinds of questions do you think an interviewer would ask? Think of possible questions and discuss them. Make a list.

1. Questions about your work experience:

a) _____

b) _____

c) _____

2. Questions about your skills:

a) _____

b) _____

c) _____

3. Questions about your education:

a) _____

b) _____

c) _____

4. Questions about your background:

a) _____

b) _____

c) _____

5. Questions about your plans for the future:

a) _____

b) _____

c) _____

6. Questions about your English:

a) _____

b) _____

c) _____

7. Questions about experience with customers:

a) _____

b) _____

c) _____

8. Questions about transportation:

a) _____

b) _____

c) _____

Quick Practice

Some interview questions are easy to answer ("Where were you born?"). Other questions are more difficult ("What is your greatest weakness?"). Sometimes the interviewer just says: "Tell me about yourself." Choose a job you would like to apply for from the list below. Then answer the questions that follow.

JOB OPPORTUNITIES:

1. *In a Hotel:* custodian, maid, bell hop, parking attendant, shuttle driver, desk clerk, restaurant worker, assistant manager

2. *In a Restaurant:* bus person, host/hostess, waiter/waitress, parking attendant (valet)

3. *In a Fast Food Restaurant:* food preparer, order taker, production leader, assistant manager

4. *In an Automotive Garage:* installer (batteries, tires, headlights), brake person, tune-up person, general mechanic, service writer, floor supervisor

5. *In a Donut Shop:* donut maker, counter person, manager

6. *At a Dry Cleaners:* clerk, manager

7. *At a Copy Store:* copy clerk, assistant manager, manager

8. *At a Convenience Store:* supply clerk, assistant manager, salesperson

9. *At a Gas Station:* attendant, mechanic, assistant manager

10. *At an Ethnic Restaurant:* kitchen helper, waiter/waitress, assistant manager

Explain what job you would like and then answer each question.

1. *Questions about Education:*
   a) What subjects did you like best in school?
   b) Which subjects did you hate?
   c) What did you learn in school?
   d) Do you plan to continue your education?

2. *Questions about Work Experience:*
   a) What was your last job like?
   b) What did you like best about your job?
   c) What did you not like about your job?
   d) Which do you like better, working alone or working with other people?
   e) What kind of boss would you like to work for?
   f) What kind of boss would you never work for?
   g) What do you expect from your co-workers?

3. *Questions about Skills:*
   a) What skills do you have that would be useful for this job?
   b) What skills do you have that would make you a good manager?
   c) Why should we hire you for this job?

4. *Interview Questions about Yourself:*
   a) Why do you want this job?
   b) What kind of person are you?
   c) What kind of person do you admire the most and why?
   d) What is most important to you in life?
   e) What is your greatest strength?
   f) What is your greatest weakness?
   g) Have you ever stolen anything?
   h) What do you like best about this country?
   i) Explain why you would be the best person for this job.

Communication Skills Practice

Generally, an employee who is looking for a new job or a better job outside of the company needs to go through an employment interview. This section will give you practice being both an interviewer (the person who offers the job) and the applicant (the person who wants the job). Use the questions on page 141 as a guide.

ROLES

One person will be the interviewer, another person will be the applicant or interviewee.

Interviewer: Talks to the applicant; explains what positions are available; asks questions; tries to find out if the applicant is qualified.

Applicant: Talks to interviewer; chooses the position that he or she would like to have; answers questions; explains why he or she is qualified to do the work.

AT AN AUTOMOTIVE REPAIRSHOP

There are two job openings: one for mechanic-in-training to do oil changes and change batteries and one for a tune-up person.

Interviewer: Asks about general work experience.
Asks about experience working with cars.
Asks if applicant has own tools.
Asks about experience dealing with customers.
Asks about knowledge of "automotive English."

Applicant: Explains where he has worked before.
Talks about ability with cars and other mechanical things.
Explains what he will do about tools.
Explains what he knows about communicating with customers.
Explains what he knows and how he plans to learn more.

1. At a Hotel

There are two job openings: one for a bellhop and one for a desk clerk.

Interviewer: Asks about general work experience.

Asks about hotel experience.

Asks about knowledge of "Hotel English."

Asks about education.

Asks about plans for the future.

Applicant: Talks about the kind of job she has done.

Explains that she has skills that are helpful in hotel work.

Talks about what she knows about hotels.

Talks about the classes she has taken that will help her be a better hotel employee.

Explains what she knows about dealing with hotel guests.

2. At a Store

There are two openings; one for a sales clerk and one for a cashier.

Interviewer: Asks about experience in sales.

Asks about other work experience.

Asks about experience with English-speaking customers.

Asks about education.

Applicant: Talks about experience with sales.

Explains skills she has that are useful in sales.

Explains what classes she has taken that would be useful in sales.

3. At a Family Restaurant
There are three job openings, one for a bus person, one for a host/hostess and one for waiter/waitress.

Interviewer: Explains job openings.

Asks about work experience in restaurant work.

Asks about general work experience.

Asks about education.

Applicant: Talks about restaurant experience or about skills he has that are helpful in restaurant work.

Talks about general work experience.

Talks about education.

Explains how he plans to take more English classes.

Explains that he knows how to communicate in English.

4. At a Fast Food Restaurant
There are two job openings: one for a counter clerk and one for an assistant manager.

Interviewer: Asks about general work experience.

Asks about experience selling food or working in a restaurant.

Asks about knowledge of "Restaurant English."

Applicant: Explains what kind of work she has done.

Explains what she knows how to do.

Talks about restaurant experience.

Explains what she has learned about communicating with customers.

Calculating Skills

Many employees get paid "by the hour." For example, a production leader at a fast food restaurant may make $5.00 an hour. If he or she works 40 hours a week, the weekly pay before taxes, is $200.

However, the production leader will not be able to take home the entire $200. The employer will deduct money for taxes from the paycheck. The production leader's "take home pay" will be quite a bit less.

Study the case of Sylvia Valdez and calculate how much money she makes "before taxes" and how much money she can take home "after taxes."

Sylvia works part-time in a fast food restaurant and makes $4.00 an hour. She works 20 hours a week. (Sylvia goes to adult school three times a week to improve her English and learn some business skills.)

Before taxes, how much does Sylvia make?

a. Per week: _____

b. Per year: _____

Sylvia's employer deducts 10% of her check for taxes. After taxes, how much money does Sylvia make?

a. Per week: _____

b. Per year: _____

After several weeks on the job, Sylvia is promoted to production manager on her shift. She now makes $4.75 an hour. She drops one of her classes at school and increases her hours from 20 hours a week to 30 hours a week. Calculate how Sylvia's situation has changed.

How much money does Sylvia now make before taxes?

a. Per week: _____

b. Per year: _____

How much more money is Sylvia now making after taxes? (The taxes are 16%.)

a. Per week: _____

b. Per year: _____

What is your opinion?

Sylvia is thinking of quitting school. Should she quit altogether, work full time, and hope to become assistant manager? Explain your reasons.

Moving Up Faster

Many service employees plan to get better jobs and move up the job ladder. Many of these employees follow this plan:

a) They continue to improve their communication skills and use every opportunity to listen, speak, read and write in English.

b) They get as much information as they can about jobs that interest them and then get the training, experience or education required for those jobs.

c) They go to a number of job interviews to get practice and improve their chances of getting the job they want.

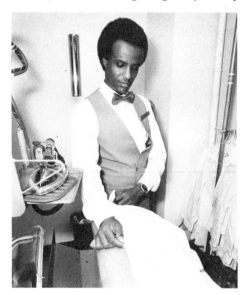 

Here are some tips to help you improve your chances for getting ahead in your career. Which of these methods have you already tried? Which do you plan on trying? Circle the answer that explains your situation.

1. I usually observe customer/employee interactions whenever I go shopping, eat out or use another kind of service. I pay careful attention to how service employees handle a situation and often make notes on what people say.

already doing it / will try this method / don't think it'll work

2. I talk a great deal with my co-workers and fellow students to show that I am friendly and interested in other people and also to get a better idea of what is going on at work.

already doing it / will try this method / don't think it'll work

3. I often talk to other people who have jobs that I would like to have and ask them about their careers. I try to find out how these people got to where they are.

already doing it / will try this method / don't think it'll work

4. I frequently ask my boss for information so that I can understand my work better. I also show interest in the company as a whole, not just in my individual job.

already doing it / will try this method / don't think it'll work

5. I sometimes make small talk with other customers, and I also talk to my neighbors and friends. Perhaps someone will have news of an exciting job opening and will let me know about it.

already doing it / will try this method / don't think it'll work

6. I always read the want ads in newspapers to see if there are any interesting job openings. I also look at advertisements for restaurants, hotels or other businesses that may be opening in my town. In addition, I read news articles on businesses that are about to open.

already doing it / will try this method / don't think it'll work

7. I sometimes fill out job applications just for practice, and I have a written record of my skills and qualifications.

already doing it / will try this method / don't think it'll work

8. I usually watch television programs and listen to the radio to improve my listening comprehension. I try to make a list of new words I hear and then use them whenever I can.

already doing it / will try this method / don't think it'll work

OUT IN THE REAL WORLD

1. Throughout the course you have observed employees who deal with the public. Answer these questions about the situations you have observed.

   a) In your opinion, what makes a successful service employee? What qualities do you like about them? How do they act? Give a specific example that you have observed.

   b) In your opinion, what kind of employees will probably never move up? What are their weaknesses? Again, give specific examples from your observations.

2. Some of your fellow students may have jobs. Talk to them and find out as much information as you can.

   a) Have they ever worked in a service-related job (either in their own country or in the U.S.)? What kind of work did they do? Who were their customers? Were there any problems with the job?

   b) Do they have friends and relatives that have worked in service-related jobs? What are their experiences?

   c) Are they planning to work in the service industry? What job would they like to have? If they can't get that job, what else would they be willing to do? Do they plan to stay in the same job or do they plan to move up? What do they plan to do to help them move up?

3. Find people who have jobs that you would like to have. Talk to them about their job. You may try some of these questions:

   a) How did the person get the job?

   b) Did he or she have any preparation for the job (training/education/experience)?

   c) Has this person been promoted on the job? Does he or she expect to be promoted in the future?

   d) What does the person like about the job? Which part of the job is difficult?

4. Talk to a representative of the service industry and find out information that interests you and can help you.

   a) What does the company do? Does the company plan to grow in the future?

   b) What kind of job openings does the company have? What are employees expected to do?

   c) What kind of people is the company looking for? How can someone prepare for a particular job?

   d) What advancement is available? Does the company provide training? What should an employee do who wants to move up?

5. Your friends and neighbors might know of job openings that they can tell you about. Explain that you are looking for a (better) job and see what suggestions they have.

   a) Do your friends and neighbors know of any job openings?

   b) Can your friends and neighbors tell you where you can get information about job openings?

6. Your town probably has several newspapers. Get as much information as you can by reading them.

    a) Look through the want ads in the paper and see what openings you can find. What are the qualifications required for each job?

    b) Look through several newspapers and see if you can find any articles that talk about food, restaurants, hotels, or other service industries. Sunday newspapers may be especially helpful. List the articles you find.

7. Most jobs require you to fill out a job application or write a resume. Practice putting information about yourself on paper.

    a) Whenever you see a Help Wanted sign, ask for an application and study the information that the company wants about you.

    b) Fill out a job application.

    c) Write a simple resume.

8. Watch television for an evening and see how much information you can pick up.

    a) Did you see any commercials that talk about restaurants, hotels, retail or grocery stores, repair services etc.?

    b) Which places or services did you see advertised?

    c) Would you like to work in one of those establishments?

9. What are your plans for the future? Where do you plan to start work? Where do you want to be in five years? In 10 years?

_____

Goal in five years: _____

_____

_____

Goal in ten years: _____

_____

10. Do you plan to get more education or special training so you can move up? What's your plan? Explain.

What are you going to do next week? _____

_____

What are you going to do next month? _____

_____

What are you going to do in the next five years? _____

_____